OTHER TITLES IN THE CODENOTES SERIES

CodeNotes for J2EE: EJB, JDBC, JSP, and Servlets

CodeNotes for XML

CodeNotes for .NET

CodeNotes for Java: Intermediate and Advanced Language Features

CodeNotes for VB.NET

CodeNotes® for Web-Based UI

Edited by GREGORY BRILL

CodeNotes®
for Web–Based UI

RANDOM
HOUSE

NEW YORK

Copyright © 2001 by Infusion Development Corporation

All rights reserved under International and Pan-American Copyright Conventions. Published in the United States by Random House, Inc., New York, and simultaneously in Canada by Random House of Canada Limited, Toronto.

RANDOM HOUSE TRADE PAPERBACKS and colophon are trademarks of Random House, Inc.

CodeNotes® is a registered trademark of Infusion Development Corporation.

Windows, VBScript, Jscript, and Internet Expolorer are trademarks of Microsoft Corporation.

Netscape Navigator is a trademark of AOL/Time Warner.

Java is a trademark of Sun Microsystems.

Library of Congress cataloging-in-publication data is available.

ISBN 0-8129-9216-4

Website address: www.atrandom.com

Printed in the United States of America on acid-free paper.

24689753

First Edition

Using CodeNotes

PHILOSOPHY

The CodeNotes philosophy is that the core concepts of any technology can be presented succinctly. The product of many years of consulting and training experience, the CodeNotes series is designed to make you productive in a technology in as short a time as possible.

CODENOTES POINTERS

Throughout the book, you will encounter CodeNotes pointers: ⟿UI010101. These pointers are links to additional content available on-line at the CodeNotes website. To use a CodeNotes pointer, simply point a web browser to www.codenotes.com and enter the pointer number. The website will direct you to an article or an example that provides additional information about the topic.

CODENOTES STYLE

The CodeNotes series follows certain style guidelines:

- Code objects and code keywords are highlighted using a special font. For example, array[3].

- Code blocks, screen output, and command lines are placed in individual blocks with a special font:

```
//This is an example code block
```

Listing Chapter# .X Some code

WHAT YOU NEED TO KNOW BEFORE CONTINUING

This book is intended for software developers or web designers who have a basic understanding of HTML and are generally familiar with the basic concepts of functional programming. Familiarity with at least one programming language or development environment should be sufficient. For nontechnical readers, the UI theory portion of Chapter 3 has no prerequisites.

About the Authors

GREGORY BRILL is president of Infusion Development Corporation, a firm specializing in architecting global securities trading and analytic systems for several of the world's largest investment banks situated in the United States and Tokyo. He has written articles for *C++ Users Journal,* and he is the author of *Applying COM+.* He lives in New York City.

CRAIG WILLS is a writer and researcher for Infusion Development Corporation. He has worked in technical documentation at a variety of institutions in both Canada and the United States, including major banks, Internet consulting firms, and software component development companies. In his spare time, Craig enjoys competitive swimming, punk and ska music, and writing fiction. Craig currently lives in Niagara-on-the-Lake, Ontario.

DAVID ORR works as a consultant for Infusion Development Corporation. He has developed software for financial institutions, digital-media corporations, and the medical imaging industry in both the United States and Canada. David enjoys life on the volleyball beach-tour, playing guitar, and producing music. He currently lives in New York City.

Contributing Authors

RYAN RING manages the creative department at Open-i Media in New York City, where he is also an ongoing contributor to curriculum development for Open-i training. His background includes video production, editing, broadcast design, and streaming media.

MICHAEL VAN ATTER is a software consultant with Infusion Development Corporation. He specializes in web development, and has worked on some of the most popular Canadian news websites and e-commerce sites. Michael has also consulted for large financial institutions. He was born in Canada and still lives in Oakville, Ontario, where he enjoys racing his car at Mosport International Raceway and playing hockey and football.

More information about the authors and Infusion Development Corporation can be found at www.infusiondev.com/codenotes.

Acknowledgments

First, thanks to John Gomez who saw the potential of the CodeNotes idea before anyone else and introduced me to Random House. Without John, there would be no CodeNotes. I'd also like to thank Annik La-Farge, who fearlessly championed the series and whose creativity, enthusiasm, and publishing savvy have been instrumental in its creation. Thank you to Mary Bahr, our unflappable editor, who paved the way and crafted the marketing. Thank you to Ann Godoff whose strength, decisiveness, and wisdom gave CodeNotes just the momentum it needed. And, of course, the production, sales, and business teams at Random House, with particular thanks to Howard Weill, Jean Cody, and Richard Elman.

On the Infusion Development side, thank you to Rob McGovern for his dedication to the CodeNotes series and help in preparing this installment. Thank you to the CodeNotes reviewers, who gave us invaluable feedback and suggestions on our early drafts. And thank you to the entire cast and crew of Infusion Development Corporation, who have supported and encouraged this venture throughout, with special thanks to Irene Wilk-Dominique, Jessica Pollack, and DeBorah Johnson, who helped administrate and manage so much of this process. I know Code-Notes was extremely trying, tough to do, and involved an awesome amount of research, writing, and editing. But here it is . . . as we envisioned it.

Gregory Brill

Contents

CodeNotes® for Web-Based UI

Chapter 1

—

INTRODUCTION

Orientation

The Purpose of this CodeNote

A chasm exists between software developers and website designers. This is unfortunate, because the skill sets of these two groups overlap in many ways: designers may need to understand programming to add interactivity to their sites, and developers need to understand how browsers and HTML operate to leverage the Web in their applications. This CodeNote is intended to create a bridge between these two skill sets; specifically, it provides a common methodology of user interface (UI) design for creating effective websites (or web-based UIs for applications). Chapter 3 distills the many contemporary theories of web design into some rules of thumb that can be employed to create good-looking and highly functional web design. The remaining chapters give the reader (software developer or website designer) a working understanding of the primary web technologies and languages; they include tutorials on the languages and technologies required to add a dynamic dimension and interactivity to web pages.

Web UI Design Theory

While one may be familiar with the technologies and development languages of web design, to use them effectively one needs to understand the rules of design by which an effective and aesthetically pleasing web UI is put together. We say "rules of design" because, contrary to the beliefs of many developers, making a good UI is not a purely creative act. By virtue of understanding certain rules of color, layout, and font (outlined in Chapter 3), one can actually take a somewhat algorithmic approach to web design.

The choice of colors is, for example, not just a matter of opinion: different colors at different saturations, graduations, and relationships to one another on the color wheel (see Chapter 3) create different feels. There are rules for what colors are complementary to one another and in what ratio they should be used together. Similarly, there are definitively good and bad placements for navigation and some absolute do's and don'ts in terms of how data, navigation, and images are laid out.

After covering basic design theory, these CodeNotes will introduce the technologies of web development. The "Summary" and "Design Notes" sections of these chapters will relate the technologies being introduced to the UI chapter (Chapter 3); these will provide a UI context to which the technologies being introduced may be specifically applied.

The Web UI Technologies

While there may seem to be a myriad of technologies associated with client-side web UI, there are, in actuality, only a few we need to be concerned with. In this book we will explore DHTML/CSS, JavaScript, some advanced HTML (the reader is advised to have a basic understanding of HTML prior to reading this CodeNote), XML, and XSLT. Often these technologies work together, but it can be difficult to understand where one leaves off and another picks up, or where different technologies might be used to accomplish the same thing. To make matters more challenging, major browsers, while supporting the same technologies, may support them in slightly different ways with differing levels of compatibility. Even different versions of the *same* browser may render things differently.

While additional effort is required to make certain that your UI functions similarly in Internet Explorer, Netscape, and other browsers (many differences will be addressed in the appendix to this book), it is not an insurmountable problem. Fortunately, at the time of this writing, the industry has largely converged on a few standard web-UI technologies that major web browsers implement. They are:

- *HTML.* The HyperText Markup Language is the foundation technology of web UI. At its most basic level, HTML consists of an established (presently version 4.01, www.w3c.org) set of tags and attributes defining how a browser should display a document. The data itself takes the form of the text held between a given pair of formatting tags. HTML is the basis for all web UI, but has two significant drawbacks: (1) it mixes presentation and formatting information with data, making the two very tedious to separate when required, and (2) HTML, by itself, is an entirely fixed format by the time it arrives at a browser; it displays like the static page of a printed book. A displayed HTML page does not have any dynamic or changeable qualities that graphically react to the user's interaction with the page.

• *DHTML*. You can think of Dynamic HTML as an enhancement to your browser that enables dynamic web behavior *after* your page has loaded (for example, changing color when the user moves a mouse over some part of the page). As we will see in Chapter 5, DHTML by itself is not capable of making a web page interactive; rather, it requires two additional elements with which it must work in concert. The first DHTML requirement is that the host browser must support a Document Object Model (DOM), which is a programmatically accessible (and changeable) representation of a web page. A browser that supports DHTML must necessarily support a DOM (though the DOMs may be slightly different with different browsers; see the appendix for details). The second DHTML requirement is that a scripting language (typically JavaScript) be present to respond to events (perhaps the user mouses-over DHTML-identified regions of HTML) and then manipulate the page in some way to affect these regions.

• *Cascading Style Sheets (CSS)*. CSS is considered part of DHTML, but you can think of it as having a life of its own as well. CSS is predominately a mechanism for taking a group of HTML formats and styles that are frequently used together and grouping them into classes. When a particular grouping of formats is required (for example, in a hypothetical News website, there may be certain formatting and style tags that make up a news headline) for which a CSS class exists (i.e., the class News-Headline is 20 point, bold, italic, and red), the HTML page can succinctly reference the class to specify the format of some text. This is far easier and more efficient than restating the disparate formatting and style tags every time a news headline is needed.

• *JavaScript*. Despite its name, the JavaScript language itself is neither a derivative of nor is it related to Java. Originally drawn from a Netscape specification known as "LiveScript," Sun and Netscape have rebranded their implementation as "JavaScript." JavaScript in the form of the ECMAScript standard, has since become the established client-side scripting language; it is used to manipulate the browser's DOM so as to create dynamic effects on otherwise static web pages for all browsers.

- *XML.* Extensible Markup Language represents any kind of textual data as a tree-like hierarchy in a text file. The data of an XML document is kept between start and end tags similar to HTML, but, unlike HTML, these tags can be named whatever the designer wishes; they have no predefined meaning. While an XML document looks similar to an HTML document (both have tags and attributes, and both keep their data between these tags), basic XML has *nothing* to do with presentation and makes no assumptions that it will ever be viewed by a browser. XML is becoming the standard for transporting information between different systems and, as we will see in Chapter 6, XML documents can easily be transformed into HTML pages via a technology known as XSLT.
- *XSLT.* XSLT is actually an XML grammar that specifies how an XML document that contains tags and data may be translated into some other textual form. While XSLT may specify any output format, it is often used to translate XML documents into HTML documents. This XML-to-XSLT transformation process provides for the long-sought-after split between data and presentation that the industry has been looking for.

If you are not familiar with some of the technologies listed here, don't worry; this CodeNote will demonstrate where, when, and how they can be used.

Battle of the Browsers: Developing for the Lowest (or Highest) Common Denominator

There is a saying in this industry: "The nice thing about standards is that there are so many to choose from." This wry comment is definitely applicable to web UI. Fortunately or unfortunately (depending on your point of view), web developers work in an exponentially growing market dominated by the browser duopoly of Netscape (more specifically, AOL/Time Warner) and Microsoft. The two companies have run a neck-to-neck race since 1995 and, at different times, have leapfrogged each other with new interactive/dynamic features and capabilities.

While new features are always welcome, it puts developers and designers in a difficult spot when one browser supports a feature that another does not. It is even more frustrating when both browsers support a similar feature, but have slightly different, subtly incompatible approaches. All in all, the use of any feature above the HTML 3.2 (we are at 4.1 at the time of this writing) specification inevitably gives rise to the possibility that there are some people using older browsers that will not be able to utilize the feature. Or, worse yet, the feature may actually be disruptive to browsers that do not know how to accommodate it. These sorts of issues are particularly noticeable with DHTML and the Document Object Model (DOM).

At the time of this writing, many developers would argue that Microsoft's Internet Explorer (IE) has taken a strong lead over Netscape. IE supports a rich, fully featured (and backward-compatible) DOM, enhanced JavaScript features, and intrinsic support for basic XML and XSLT. For its part, Netscape has completely broken with its technological strategies of the past. It has leaped out of its 4.x version series and into version 6.0 (there was no version 5.0), where, like IE 5.x, it (partially) implements a specification from The World Wide Web Consortium (W3C; www.w3c.org), DOM Level 1. But at a cost. Whereas IE remained backward-compatible with its non–DOM Level 1 methodologies, Netscape chose to completely break with its past and not support its previous proprietary approaches.

At any rate, it might seem that with both IE 6 and Netscape 6 supporting the W3C DOM Level 1 (and thereby, at long last, having similar dynamic capabilities) we finally have a common platform to write to. Unfortunately, at the time of this writing, Netscape 6.0 adoption has been slow. Furthermore, many major corporations with controlled, centralized releases of software (browsers included) are still standardized on Netscape 4.x. What's more, they will be very likely to consider deploying IE in the future as opposed to Netscape 6, even if they have been traditional Netscape users; the two-year delay between Netscape releases 4 and 6 has, arguably, allowed Microsoft's aggressive marketing and development tactics (and jump start on many new features) to eat into Netscape's install-base. However, while a number of Netscape users have switched to IE, many others will remain loyal to Netscape—they may feel it is a superior technology, they may be philosophically opposed to Microsoft, or they may be familiar with it and simply prefer Netscape. It is important to point out, though, that many Netscape loyalists will stick with a version of Netscape 4.x as opposed to adopting 6.0. Here again, they may prefer the older versions because they are familiar with them, or it may be a corporate standard where they work. So, you have, in essence, Netscape 4.x versus IE 5.x (and soon IE 6). The difficulty here is that there are fundamental differences between these two browsers. Netscape 4.x leverages a proprietary technology for dynamically modifying web pages via a scripting interface known as Layers; IE has never supported Layers. However, not only have Layers been cast aside in Netscape 6.0 in favor of the DOM Level 1 specification, but

Netscape 6.0 will not even recognize Layer syntax from older versions of itself.

So where does all this leave us? After reading this CodeNote and ramping up on web design theory and the primary web technologies, will you be able to apply what you learned? Or will you be forever forced to develop and design for the lowest common denominator?

XML and XSLT to the Rescue?

In the final analysis, there is no easy way to avoid coding a sophisticated web UI differently (at least slightly) to accommodate different browsers. At the very least, developers must test their functionality with different browsers and modify or perhaps eliminate those approaches and features that do not operate properly across browser vendors and versions. And so either you end up with multiple versions of your web application or you need to dumb down that application so that "one size fits all" for every browser. However, new developments in XML and XSLT may make the first option (multiple versions) more palatable and less work than it has traditionally been.

In the last couple of years, XML has certainly gotten a lot of attention. XML, by itself, is a simple text markup language; it uses name-value pairs of the form `<someElement>Your data</someElement>` in a hierarchical way (i.e., the value of a name-value pair can be the parent of another name-value pair) similar to the way an HTML page does. What is powerful about XML is not so much the grammar itself but the ancillary tools and technologies that can be used in conjunction with XML, one of which can help us solve our cross-browser problem.

On November 16, 1999, the W3C specification for XSLT reached recommendation status, indicating the W3C's support for the specification. We will discuss XSLT in greater detail in Chapter 6, but for now you can think of it as a simple text document that describes how a given XML document may be translated into an HTML document. (In reality, an XSLT file can specify translations other than HTML, but we are trying to keep things simple for the moment.) An XML-to-HTML translation is more than just a neat trick; it allows you to completely separate your data and your presentation logic. This is significant, because your data never changes to suit the browser; only the presentation logic does. So if we design our web-based tier to produce XML documents as opposed to HTML (this is not as difficult as you might imagine; see "Using XML and XSLT to Support All Browser Versions" in Chapter 6), we can have a small set of XSLT files—one for each browser—that your system can call on to translate XML into the HTML/DHTML/JavaScript as appropriate for the requesting browser.

While it is true that you must still maintain different XSLT files to support the different browsers, this is far less effort and aggravation than maintaining entirely different websites consisting of a complete set of HTML page variations for each different browser. It is also simpler than writing or maintaining ASP, JSP, or CGI code that dynamically creates different HTML depending on the calling browser.

In Chapter 6, we will introduce one possible strategy for leveraging features available on the most recent version of browsers, but gracefully degrading to older versions—and all without writing additional code.

LAYOUT OF THIS CODENOTE

This CodeNote will explore:

- Chapter 1, "Introduction." You are here.
- Chapter 2, "Installation." This chapter will discuss the installation of the software and tools you may want to use while working through this CodeNote. Installation notes on Netscape, Internet Explorer, and Opera are provided, with additional coverage of the ancillary tools and technologies the reader may find useful, such as XML/XSLT compilers, HTML editors, and imaging software.
- Chapter 3, "User Interface Design Theory." Contemporary theories of web-based UI design are distilled in this chapter. Optimal layout, color theory, design, navigation, font selection, and many other topics will be explored. Additionally, this chapter includes a website makeover: using the design rules outlined, a nonoptimal site is made into one that is both functional and aesthetically pleasing.
- Chapter 4, "JavaScript." JavaScript has emerged as the predominant client-side scripting language for all major browsers. This chapter provides a complete tutorial on the language and its constructs, as well as how it can be interlaced with HTML to add programmatic capabilities to web pages.
- Chapter 5, "DHTML and the Document Object Model." Dynamic HTML groups a few different technologies together, including Cascading Style Sheets (CSS), JavaScript, and the Document Object Model (DOM). This chapter will explore these different technologies and how they work together under the DHTML moniker to provide dynamic, responsive, and sophisticated client-side pages.
- Chapter 6, "XML-XSLT." XML and XSLT provide many ways to drastically simplify the development of applications that must

operate cross-browser. This chapter will demonstrate how standard XSLT transforms may be set up to translate simple XML documents to nicely formatted HTML/DHTML documents.

- Chapter 7, "Tables." Tables are vitally important in HTML. They form the basis of many web page layouts, and are the de facto method for displaying tabular data. This chapter will explore complex tables and introduce some DHTML techniques for sophisticated table manipulation and visual effects.

- Chapter 8, "Trees and Menus." Tables are useful for displaying tabular data, but trees are the structure of choice for hierarchical data. This chapter explores how data trees and dynamic tree-like navigation structures can be created with HTML and DHTML. The anatomy of DHTML-based dynamic pop-up menus will also be explored.

- Appendix. Netscape and Internet Explorer have very different support for different features throughout their version histories. This appendix describes and charts all the functional differences for every version of these different browsers.

Chapter 2

—

INSTALLATION

The only prerequisite software for this CodeNote is a browser and a text editor. This chapter will, however, give you an introduction to the different browser versions available to you and a number of tools that can speed up your web development.

Installing any of the browsers and tools discussed in this chapter is, for the most part, straightforward. Unless otherwise noted, the programs download as self-extracting applications with a setup program.

Note that because web links can change at any time without notice (and can be cumbersome to type) we provide CodeNotes pointers. Jumping to the CodeNotes pointer will bring you to the links page within the CodeNotes website. The links page contains the most current links to the downloadable components.

BROWSERS

This CodeNote focuses predominately on Netscape's Navigator and Microsoft's Internet Explorer (IE). Many of the examples and techniques illustrated in this CodeNote require a relatively recent version of either Netscape or IE—specifically, Netscape versions 4.x or 6.x and IE 5.X or higher.

- *Netscape 4.x/6.x.* At the time of this writing, Netscape's current version is 6.x. Unfortunately, Netscape 6.x is not fully compatible with Netscape 4.x versions. Specifically, Netscape has abandoned a proprietary dynamic technology (Layers) in favor of a W3C specification (DOM Level 1). Adoption of Netscape 6.x has been slow, however, and there are still a good number of Netscape 4.x users on the Web. You may, therefore, want to install multiple versions of Netscape side by side to make certain that your web design and development functions correctly on all relevant Netscape versions. For download links to various Netscape versions on different operating systems, see ⟳UI020001.

- *Microsoft IE 5.x, 6 (beta)*. At the time of this writing, IE 6 is in beta release. Unlike Netscape, multiple IE versions do not easily coexist on the same machine. This is partially because IE does not install as a traditional executable application compiled for a particular operating system, but rather as an ActiveX component that many Windows applications (of which the browser is only one) rely on. While ActiveX components are restricted to Microsoft platforms (and the Macintosh OS in a limited way), they do allow any Windows application to embed the IE browser and use it for their own display purposes. Windows help, for example, is based on the IE ActiveX component. The IE browser itself is only a shell, a relatively simple form that embeds the IE ActiveX component. For links to downloads of IE for Windows and Macintosh, go to ⟳UI020002.

HTML/DHTML EDITORS

All that is needed to develop a sophisticated website is a text editor. Certain tools can, however, speed up your development and even generate scripting code to add interactivity to your web pages. Some popular tools are:

- *Macromedia Dreamweaver*. Dreamweaver is a WYSIWYG (What You See Is What You Get) HTML editor that allows you to create complex web pages via drag and drop. It even "componentizes" certain functionality (such as menus) and will generate client-side scripting automatically. It is a popular tool, and an educational one as well: the novice web developer can study the HTML and DHTML code Dreamweaver produces to learn how certain effects operate. Links to trial downloads of Dreamweaver can be found at ⟳UI020003.

- *Microsoft FrontPage*. Like Dreamweaver, FrontPage is a WYSIWYG HTML editor. FrontPage, however, leverages certain Microsoft-specific conventions and targets a Microsoft IIS (Internet Information Server) or Personal Web Server platform for deployment. If you are working within a Microsoft web back-end framework, FrontPage is ideal. However, if you are working with a different web server, FrontPage might be considered superfluous. For links to more information about FrontPage, see ⟳UI020004.

- *Microsoft Visual InterDev.* The InterDev environment is better suited for the experienced web developer than FrontPage, which seems to favor the novice, Microsoft-centric web developer. It offers WYSIWYG capability and also features Microsoft's IntelliSense, so it will automatically pop up JavaScript property names as you write code. This feature can save the novice user from needing to constantly jump to a reference. Generally, Inter-Dev is a useful tool, and if you have installed Microsoft's Visual Studio 6.0 you already own it. Links to more information on Visual InterDev can be found at ⟳UI020005.

GRAPHIC EDITORS

There is no rule that a website must use images. However, images can contribute greatly to the feel of a site and, from a practical point of view, they are often used to create navigation bars, menus, and other key components of a site. Although this CodeNote does not cover creation or design of web graphics, the following tools are very useful for creating and editing graphics for the Web.

- *Adobe Photoshop.* This is the de facto standard for graphic designers. It is not a program for beginners. However, fluency with this program will enable users to achieve any graphical effect they can envision. Links to trial versions of Photoshop can be found at ⟳UI020006.
- *Xara X.* This is a relatively inexpensive graphical design program that gives Adobe Photoshop a run for its money as it applies to creating graphics for the Web. It has a very simple interface not unlike that of Microsoft's Paintbrush, and it seems specifically geared to creating graphics and effects for the Web, where Adobe may seem to be a more general graphical package. Links to trial versions of Xara X can be found at ⟳UI020007.

XSLT PROCESSORS

In Chapter 6 we introduce XML and XSLT and discuss a strategy for leveraging these technologies to target multiple browser versions. You may want to read Chapter 6 first, and then return to this section.

To transform XML to another XML format or a non-XML format (for example, translating an XML file to an HTML page), you'll need an *XSLT processor*. There are many different XSLT processors available, and they normally come bundled with XML parsers and other functionality. For the purposes of this CodeNote, you can get adequate experience with XML using a simple text editor, and we recommend the following command line XSLT processor:

- *The SAXON XSLT Processor (Java and Win32)*. Michael Kay's SAXON is one of the earliest XSLT 1.0–compliant processors, and it includes its own embedded XML SAX parser. Both Java-based and Windows-executable versions are available (see ⚓UI020008). If you are not planning to develop with SAXON and simply want a stand-alone Win32 XSLT processor to perform XML translations via command line, you can download *Instant Saxon*. This utility is usable from the command line.

Chapter 3

USER INTERFACE DESIGN THEORY

This book introduces a wide variety of technologies that can be used to design attractive, functional, and highly usable web user interfaces. Unfortunately, these same technologies can also be applied incorrectly and otherwise misused to create incredibly bad user interfaces. Before using JavaScript, DHTML, XSLT, or any of the other tools introduced in subsequent chapters, you need to understand some basics about what works and what doesn't on the Web.

Most Web users will have a mental list of websites they like and websites to which they will never go back. You know your favorite news sites and shopping sites, and you use them not only because they provide good services, but because they are efficient and convenient. But do you know why? Do you know why one website satisfies you, while another frustrates you? Although sometimes the mistakes made by website authors are obvious, like an excess of banner advertisements or a complex frame structure, other irritations are more subtle. An e-commerce site may be *uncomfortable* for users because of nonstandard button placement, clashing (or too subtle) color schemes, unnecessary page refreshes, or difficulty identifying required fields. All of these items affect both the look and feel and the navigability of the website, which, in turn, affect user satisfaction.

This chapter will attempt to shed some light on these subtleties by providing a series of general rules and practices that you should follow when creating a web user interface for your application. Although many of these rules apply to web pages in general, or even to entire websites, this chapter is specifically geared toward user interfaces for web-based services, such as shopping, finance management, and customer service. You will find that applying the rules set out here when creating your web user interface will result in a much more usable and attractive site than would simply applying the technologies you have already learned without considering the finer nuances of web usability.

SIMPLE APPLICATION

This chapter begins with the relatively broad topic of page layout and moves into more specific topics as it progresses. The simple application shown here is a page from a fictional developer code-sharing website called Craig's Code Cove. This site, as presented in the figures throughout this chapter, provides content in the form of code examples and computer advice. As such, the site should be easy to navigate and devote most of the page to the actual content. Figure 3.1 is an example of a badly designed web user interface. The examples in each topic of this chapter will improve upon this interface by applying the rules discussed in the particular topic. By the end of the chapter, the badly designed interface will have evolved into a well-organized, highly usable interface that is a good example of how a website should look. The progressive nature of the examples should demonstrate the improvements produced by applying the rules of web user interface theory.

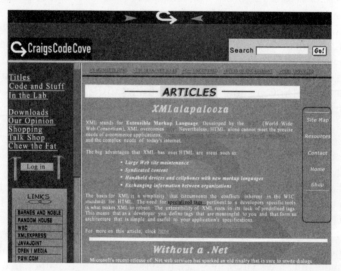

Figure 3.1   Badly designed web user interface

Some of the many things wrong with this user interface include too much space dedicated to navigation and title bars, poor heading and link names, disorganized navigation, unreadable text, bad choice of color scheme, and too many large images (including an incredibly time-wasting background image behind the body text). All of these issues and more will be addressed as we progress through this chapter. You can see a color version of this page at CodeNotes pointer ⌐**CN**⤷UI030001.

CORE CONCEPTS

Before discussing interface design, we'll mention a few critical rules that always apply when producing content or applications for the Web. These rules should be adhered to no matter what you are trying to do.

Don't Break Familiar Things
Do not change the appearance or functionality of familiar browser controls. Although modern web technologies can allow you to make your scrollbars and menus interesting colors and shapes, you must understand that these items have evolved over time to become standardized *idioms*. That is, they are metaphors (in this case, navigational metaphors) that people have come to identify with specific functionality. Thus, the "cool factor" of changing them is often outweighed by the extra time users must take to figure out what does what. Make sure your site's form always has clear and practical function. What is really cool is interesting design elements that are also instantly understandable.

In addition, the two most commonly used web navigation tools (hyperlinks and the Back button) should not be broken for the sake of interesting effects. The blue color of unvisited hyperlinks is a web-wide convention, and if this convention is broken it can cause confusion for web users trying to figure out where they have been and where they can go. The Back button should always move users back to the page from which they have just come; forcing an instant redirect to another page (using JavaScript) on your site when users hit the Back button is confusing and irritating.

The general rule: People have come to expect certain conventions on the Web, and you should use caution not to veer too far from them. Don't break familiar things simply for the sake of appearance.

Don't Try to Control Your User's Browser
There are many ways in which you can use client-side JavaScript or CSS stylesheets to control how users view your page or how their browsers look. With a few exceptions (such as opening a new small window to

provide instructions on the current page), this is a bad idea. Most users have their browsers a certain size for a reason, and many have set their own color schemes (possibly because they have difficulty seeing certain colors). If you attempt to force your own preferences upon them, they will probably not be happy and may not come back to your site. You should design your web user interface in such a way that it can conform to the browser settings of the majority of users.

Some general don'ts:

- Don't try to force users to go places they don't want to go, either by opening new browser windows or redirecting them to other pages. In other words, you should navigate to a new page only on a specific user request.
- Don't change the size of their browser windows, or remove the toolbars and status bars they have configured in their browsers.
- Don't force bookmarks or favorites into their browsers.
- Don't make them download new technologies like Flash or Shockwave just to use your website. If you choose to use a plug-in or player technology, be sure to give users the choice of an HTML alternative.
- Don't use the !important CSS attribute, which allows you to force an override of the user's style preferences.

Optimize Wait Times

Your goal should be to keep your page sizes as small as possible, so that your users have minimal time to wait between clicking and getting a result. According to Jakob Nielsen (author of *Designing Web Usability,* New Riders Publishing, Indianapolis, IN, 1999), 10 seconds is the maximum wait time any user should have for a page. Any longer than this, and you are losing your user's attention. A 1-second wait time is optimal, but rarely achievable. If you have graphics-intensive or otherwise byte-heavy pages, make sure you warn users that they will have to wait longer than usual.

A good maximum weight for a web page is 70 KB. As high as 100 KB is acceptable, although users with slower connections may experience delays. Links to pages larger than 100 KB should indicate the size and expected download time of the page at low bandwidth. Remember that these numbers are *maximums.* Smaller pages will load faster, which is better if it can be done without sacrificing appearance.

One strategy for optimizing wait times is to cache part or all of your content. There are many different caching strategies, which are beyond the scope of this book. For more on caching, see ⌀**CN**◝UI030015.

Cultural Assumptions

The rules in this CodeNote are not universal. Although many of them will apply to anyone designing in any country, some of the rules presented here may be Anglo-centric. Since this book is written in English and was published in North America, all the rules will apply to western developers. If you are reading this book and developing web pages in a country outside of North America, keep in mind that some rules may be different for your culture. For example, for Hebrew speakers, many elements of page layout will be reversed, since Hebrew is read from right to left instead of left to right. We will try to indicate when rules are obviously geared toward English speakers.

Internationalization is an extensive topic covering everything from page orientation to icon selection. Creating a website that is truly international requires a significant effort in terms of language, design, layout, and functionality. For a more thorough introduction to internationalization, see ⚭UI030016.

Topic: Page Layout

The organization of a web page is evident primarily in its page layout. Although fonts, colors, and other considerations do make an impact and often improve usability, it is the location of key items within the browser that will make a site easy or difficult to use. This topic will cover various subjects in page layout and organization, and provide some rules and recommendations that should help you arrange your page for optimal usability.

CONCEPTS

Screen Real Estate

"Screen real estate" refers to the amount of space each element of a web page takes up on the screen. Common elements that take up significant amounts of real estate include text or form content (the bulk of the page), navigation (usually in bars at the sides or top of the page), headers and footers, and advertisements. Though it is usually obvious that content should constitute the bulk of a page, it is not always easy to tell exactly how much of the page this entails.

Choose Your Audience's Screen Resolution

Your audience's display resolution greatly influences how you design your site. Most likely, a user's resolution will be set at 800×600 or 1024×768 pixels. However, computers with older monitors may be set to display as low as 640×480. You should decide the minimum resolution to which you want to target your website before starting to design it. At the time of this writing, we recommend 800×600, as lower resolutions are becoming rather uncommon. According to a February 2001 poll by statmarket.com, 89 percent of web surfers are using screen resolutions of 800×600 or above.

The higher the user's resolution, the smaller the elements of the page will appear on his or her screen. Your page may appear to lose visual quality when displayed at a lower resolution. A good idea is to design your site with your computer set at the minimum resolution that you have chosen for your audience, even if you normally use a higher (or lower) resolution. Note that it is also best to design with a color depth of 256 colors, as browsers only guarantee support for 216 web-safe colors. We will discuss web-safe colors in the "Colors" topic, later in this chapter.

Be Resolution Independent

Although you will create your page with a minimum resolution in mind (such as 800×600), always design to accommodate other screen resolutions and browser sizes. Relative and absolute sizes for tables and frames each have pros and cons in regard to this.

Absolute sizes virtually ensure that your website layout will have the same dimensions as you intended. You can assign absolute widths to elements using HTML attributes (`width` and `height`) and you can assign absolute positions to elements using CSS properties (`position:absolute` accompanied by `top` and `left` values). However, absolute sizes force site elements to remain fixed. Parts of your site may not be seen by users with lower screen resolutions or by users who do not maximize their browser windows. Thus, absolute sizes may force your users to scroll horizontally to reach parts of your page, which can be annoying.

Relative sizes, in contrast, allow tables and frames to contract or expand to accommodate users' browser and resolution preferences. Relative sizes, however, can also disrupt your layout at smaller browser resolutions (by compressing tables and frames too far), inadvertently creating a more difficult experience for your user. In reduced-size browsers, relative font and cell sizes can cause paragraphs and tables to break apart. This, however, may be an acceptable trade-off for the advantage of resolution independence.

Absolute pixel sizes should be strongly considered for table cells that contain both images and absolute text. Navigation menus often use absolute sizes when the menu's structural stability is extremely critical. When using relative widths and positions, test thoroughly at various browser window sizes to be sure that elements do not unacceptably disrupt your layout.

Content Is Key

There are many sites on the Web that contain so many advertisements, banners, and navigation tools that content seems like an afterthought. If you see this happening with your own website, remember what you are creating it for—to provide content and functionality (in the case of a web application) to your users. The content should encompass, by far, the largest portion of your user's screen.

On the other hand, you shouldn't make the screen all content and ignore navigation. As a general rule, try to make 80 percent of your page content and 20 percent navigation. Advertising and other extraneous information (such as static title bars) take away from the content of your site, and should be kept to a minimum where possible.

Note that the percentages mentioned are somewhat wishful thinking. The structure and complexity of many sites will not always allow you to stick to these rules.

How to Divide Your Screen

There are two major ways in which you can carve up your users' windows into the portions you want: tables and frames. The most common method is to use tables. Tables without borders can be used to create columns and headers on a screen. They do not necessarily have to be obvious; many sites make heavy use of tables that you would never know were there unless you thought about it or looked at the source HTML. For example, the HTML in Listing 3.1 would create a page layout with a top bar and two columns (a thin one on the left and a wide one making up the remainder of the page).

```
<html>
  <body>
    <table width="100%">
      <tr height="100" width="100%">
      <td colspan="2">Top Row</td></tr>
      <tr>
        <td width="15%">Left Column</td>
        <td width="85%">Right Column</td>
      </tr>
```

```
    </table>
  </body>
</html>
```

Listing 3.1   HTML to create a simple table-based screen layout

The other alternative for arranging your web pages is frames, which are used to divide your window into subwindows. Frames are discussed in their own section later in this topic.

A third alternative is to use <div> and <span> tags (discussed in Chapter 8). These tags provide greater flexibility than a table in terms of arranging a page by grouping elements. However, using <div> and <span> tags exclusively often results in HTML that is less readable and more difficult to maintain than a simple table structure.

Navigation Tools

Typically, your most important navigation tools should appear at the top of the page or on the top left of the page. This is the first place that English-speaking users will look when they arrive at a web page, since they read left to right, top to bottom.

Top (Horizontal) Menus

Menus at the top of a window are often static throughout a website (i.e., they exist and are the same on every page) and are used to move between very general areas. An example of this would be a site like Amazon.com, where the top menu bar is used to move among sections such as books, music, electronics, and video. Top menus should be located in the upper 10 to 15 percent of the window.

Left (Vertical) Menus

Menus appearing at the left side of a page are often dynamic; that is, they change depending on the user's actions. Typically, left-side menus contain options pertaining to the specific page you are on, rather than the website as a whole. These menus are arranged vertically and, as a general rule, the most important or most popular tools or links should appear at the top of the menu. This allows users, particularly those with small browser windows, to avoid having to scroll down to find the options they need. You should generally keep menu options to a minimum, but collapsible tree menus in particular may become long depending on the nature of your site; therefore, you should make sure they are organized in an efficient manner. If you are using tree menus, try to have the hierarchy of the tree mirror the hierarchy of your website; if you do this, users will only rarely need to expand more than two parts of the tree at a time.

Other Menu Locations

In certain cases, most notably website home pages, it is useful to have more than two navigation areas on a page. For example, news sites often have a right-hand menu bar from which you can link to articles or external sites related to the article you are reading. It is also sometimes advantageous to include simple links such as "top," "next," and "home" at the bottom of a long page of text, to prevent users from having to scroll back up the page. The addition of extra navigation is rarely justifiable, however, simply because every navigation tool added to the page takes up space that could be used for content.

Forms

Forms are used in virtually every web application to gather information from users. Whether you are leveraging a simple form for searching or retrieving data from a database or a complex form for a user's personal information, there are certain rules you should follow to make form entry easier and less susceptible to error.

Tables, Not Paragraphs

Tables are the best way of organizing a page, particularly one containing entry forms. Tables allow you to ensure that certain related fields or lists will remain grouped together, regardless of the size or orientation of the user's browser. They also allow you to lay out text in columns, with blocks of text side by side. Generally, you will want to use tables without borders to divide the page without making it look like a table. Remember, using whitespace is good design.

Group Your Entry Fields by Category

Arrange the input elements in such a way that there is a logical progression from the first one to the last one. If you are taking in user information, start with the easiest information first (name, address, etc.) and then move on to information that may take more work to obtain. For example, if you require the user's driver's license number, credit card number, and bank account number, group these three things together—the user will most likely need to obtain each of these pieces of information from his or her purse or wallet, and will not want to keep putting it away and getting it out again if the entry fields are distributed throughout a form.

Arrange Entry Fields by Importance

Try to keep the most important or required information at the top of the form so that the user will pay the most attention to it and be most likely to fill it out accurately. Put any optional fields at the bottom of the form, and separate them so that they can easily be ignored should the user choose to do so. Always indicate whether fields are optional or required by adding an appropriate indicator (such as "REQUIRED") next to the field.

Use Appropriate Input Types

Though there are many input types that seem more interesting or useful than a plain text entry field, it is not always wise to implement them. Users on your site have become accustomed to certain types of entry form, and you should probably not change standard fields in an attempt to make them easier on the users.

For example, dividing up the address section of a user entry field into a text entry field for street number, another for street name, and a drop-down menu for the type of street (street, drive, lane, etc.) does not make form entry any easier or more comprehensive. On the contrary, a user who is used to quickly typing his or her address as "12 Birdsall Court" into a text field will not appreciate having to tab between three different entry fields to enter the same. Even if your address data will be stored in three separate fields in a database, you may want to include JavaScript or a server-side script to split up the text instead of making the user do it for you.

Put the Buttons at the Bottom Right of the Form

English-speaking users read from left to right, top to bottom, so the buttons at the end of the form should generally appear at the bottom right. Of course, this can change depending on the design of your page. Choosing to center or left-justify the buttons generally will not decrease the usability of the form. In fact, some people prefer to left-justify buttons because the mouse motion from the right side to the left side of the screen is easier than moving straight down or left to right.

Most forms will generally have one or two buttons: one for OK (also possibly labeled "Yes," "Submit," or "Continue") and one for Cancel (or "No"). The positive button (OK, Yes, etc.) should be on the left, and the negative button should be on the right. Remember, it is much more common to hear the phrase "yes or no" than "no or yes." You may also have seen Clear buttons in forms that will reset all the fields and allow users to start again; these are generally not necessary and often cause problems because users tend to accidentally click on them and lose all their work.

Frames

Frames allow you to divide your users' browser windows into independent subwindows, each with their own characteristics and sets of scrollbars. Each window can also be made resizable, so users can customize the size of the frames. Frames were introduced by Netscape in version 3.0. Though frames might at first seem to be the ultimate solution for designing page layout, there are some definite drawbacks, which cause many user interface professionals to shun frame technology completely.

To create a frameset proportioned identically to the table layout shown in Listing 3.1, you could use code something like that shown in Listing 3.2.

```html
<html>
  <frameset rows="15%,*">
    <frameset cols="100%">
      <frame src="header.htm" name="header">
    </frameset>
    <frameset cols="15%,*">
      <frame src="navigate.htm" name="navigate">
      <frame src="mycontent.htm" name="main">
    </frameset>
  </frameset>
</html>
```

Listing 3.2   HTML to create a simple frame-based screen layout

Why Frames Are Good
Frames allow you to divide your screen into blocks that can change independently of one another. For example, you could have a left-side frame that contains a scrolling menu controlling a right-side (main) frame that contains your content. The menu remains static, while the content changes depending on what the user chooses from the menu.

Why Frames Are Bad
Frames break bookmarking. Users don't always want to have to come to the home page; often, they will bookmark a particular page deep within your site so that they can get back to it without having to navigate through everything else again. Because each frame has its own URL, bookmarking framed pages will often have strange and not very useful results, such as bookmarking only the navigation bar of the page, instead of the frameset for the entire page. Unless you use some kind of JavaScript workaround, users will not be able to return to a frameset using a bookmark. (This workaround can be found at ^{CN}UI030002.)

Frames break searching, both within pages and from search engines. Performing a text search within a frame-based page may return no results even if the text exists, simply because the user had the wrong frame in focus. Web search engines (such as Alta Vista or Google) may take a user to one frame of a page (like a menu bar) instead of the frameset.

Frames can render parts of your site unprintable. This is why you will occasionally see "Printable Version" icons on websites using frames, which will take you to a frameless page that will print correctly.

EXAMPLE

You'll recall the Craig's Code Cove website that we first introduced at the beginning of this chapter (Figure 3.1). In this example, we'll start making improvements to that site, moving toward a totally revamped Code Cove by the end of the chapter. The first step in our website transformation is to improve the page layout of our original ugly page. We'll show the result first (Figure 3.2), and then discuss some of the specific changes.

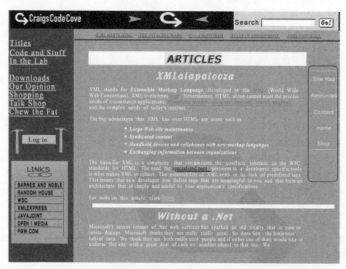

Figure 3.2   Web user interface with improved page layout

The most noticeable change here is the resizing of the top and left-side navigation and title bars to give more space to the content. We've removed a great deal of the empty black space in the top bar. Notice that we've also decided to go with a table-based layout, rather than frames. We want this website to be available to as many users as possible, so we have removed the frames to accommodate users who can't use, or don't want to use, frames.

You can see a color version of this site at CodeNotes pointer ⊶UI030003.

HOW AND WHY

How Do I Determine Which Button to Activate by Default?

JavaScript allows you to specify a button that will be active by default. If possible, the activated button should always be the most intuitive action (i.e., use the Submit button with forms). When there is not a single intuitive action to be taken after the current web page (i.e., when a button is used to determine whether or not the user wishes to join the mailing list), the button that has the least effect on the user should be activated by default (using the mailing list example, by default the user should not join the mailing list).

You can make a button the Default button by using the focus() method, as shown in Listing 3.3.

```
<form name="myForm">
  <input type="button" name="button1" value="button number 1"/>
  <input type="button" name="button2" value="button number 2"/>
  <input type="button" name="button3" value="button number 3"/>
</form>
<SCRIPT LANGUAGE="JavaScript">
<!--
  // makes button3 the default button
  document.myForm.button3.focus();
//-->
</SCRIPT>
```

Listing 3.3   Creating a Default button

DESIGN NOTES

Testing Your Web Layout

It is important to test the experience of all potential visitors to your website. In order to replicate the experiences of as many users as possible, you should test your web layout using various monitor sizes as well as various browser sizes (i.e., resizing the browser window to various dimensions). You should also test your site on different bandwidths. When creating websites, developers often have a fast local area network connection with the server hosting the computer. However, the majority of web users still have dial-up connections and, as a result, their experience will be drastically different. Finally, you should also test your site by changing the default browser settings, such as text size, to ensure you are not altering settings the user obviously prefers.

Since it can be awkward to test different browsers and settings on one machine, you might look into OS emulation. OS emulators such as VMWare and Connectix allow you to have multiple versions of an operating system (with application installs and settings) running as virtual machines *at the same time*. For more information on OS emulators, see ⟠UI030004.

SUMMARY

Page layout is the most noticeable aspect of any web page or web application. There are, fortunately, some rules of thumb you can employ to keep your layout smooth. As many elements as possible should be resolution independent. Navigation tools should take up less than 20 percent of the user's window, and should be placed in a convenient location—usually, the top and/or left of a page. Content should take up the remainder of the page, where possible. Frames can be used to further control and manipulate the arrangement of web pages, but they have some major disadvantages: frames break bookmarking, slow down page rendering, and break both in-page and search engine searching capabilities.

Topic: Content

The content of a document is the words it contains, and the arrangement and segmentation of these words. Web content is much different from printed content.

When writing a printed document, the author decides the order of the paragraphs and pages, and places them permanently in that order (possibly interspersed with images and headings). In most cases, the reader starts at the beginning of the document and reads straight through to the end.

On the Web, the control over the order in which content is read is shifted toward the reader. The reader clicks hyperlink after hyperlink, reading content only if the heading is of interest. There is no guarantee that the introduction, middle, and conclusion of a web document will be read in that order. Instead of deciding on the order of pages, web authors must decide how to divide their documents into fragments and how to use hyperlinks to connect those fragments. Knowing that web users have lower tolerance for less important material, website designers must arrange their content in such a way that users' interest is maintained and they can find exactly what they want without having to work at it.

This topic will divide web content into two categories: *microcontent* (organizational content such as headings and captions) and *macrocontent* (the actual text on the page).

CONCEPTS

Microcontent: Window Titles, Headings, and Subheadings

Users scan web pages. Very few actually take the time to read every bit of text on a given page before deciding what link to click on next. Because of this, you need to ensure that all headings and subheadings on your page are clear and meaningful. Many existing pages use amusing or clever headlines for sections of a page, attempting to draw a reader's attention. Very often, however, users will ignore any content that does not have a headline specific to what they are looking for. And if all of your headlines are obscure ("Oh What a Tangled Web We Weave") or uninformative ("Stuff"), users will go somewhere else.

Window Titles

The title of your window should change to reflect the user's present location within your website. For example, if your website is called "Wills Financial Consulting," your contact page could be titled "Contact Mr. Wills (Wills Financial Consulting)." Don't use the same title for every page, as this doesn't tell users anything about where they are. Also, window titles are what show up when users bookmark a page—if your title is vague, they may become confused and unable to find their way back.

Page Headings

Page headlines should be descriptive; avoid fluff headlines, cute headlines, or clever plays on words. "Cool New Stuff" is not a good page headline, whereas "New Downloads" is at least somewhat indicative of what the page is about and "Downloads—New Software Upgrades" is even better. Remember, headlines are often read out of context (as lists of links on other pages), so you want them to be understandable without the text that appears underneath them.

Subheadings

Remember that users are not going to read all of your pages from top to bottom, start to finish. Instead, they will scan your pages, paying attention only to sections that stand out as something they would be interested in. In order for your site to be useful, the subheadings on your page should accurately describe the text below them and should be arranged in such a way that it is immediately clear whether or not the user should pay attention to that section of the page.

Like headings, subheadings should be descriptive. Whereas a subheading such as "SIGN UP NOW!!" may call attention to itself, chances are that users will still ignore it because it doesn't contain any description of what the important text is about. "Signing Up for the gorillas.com Mailing List" is far more explicative and useful. Users who are trying to sign up for the mailing list will pay attention to this part of the page, whereas users who are not interested in the mailing list can ignore it and get on with their business.

Macrocontent: Where to Put It and How to Break It Up

Macrocontent makes up the majority of the text on the page. This is the real content of your page and is generally what users are looking for when they come to your website. Some pages, particularly those that are more web applications than web pages, will have very little macrocontent. Others, like bulletin boards and news sites, will be mostly macrocontent. No matter how much macrocontent you have, there are several rules that you should follow when writing it to ensure that users get the most out of your website.

Break Up Your Content

When writing content for the Web, make sure every paragraph or block of text introduces only one new idea, and that this idea is clarified in the first line of the paragraph. Because readers will be scanning your page rather than reading it, if they don't see what they're looking for in the first line they will most likely skip to the next paragraph.

If you have particularly long areas of text, try to break them up so that they are not on a single page. It is often much more convenient to click a Next Page button and continue reading than to have to scroll down a page to get to the rest of the text. Scrolling takes more effort and is harder on the eyes.

Try not to make your blocks of text overly wide. Users with high-resolution screens will be able to fit a lot of words on one line, but this is not necessarily a good thing. Try to arrange your page so that blocks of text have 10 to 12 words per line; any more than that, and readers' eyes will tend to wander up or down lines.

Put Important Content at the Top

If you have content that the user must scroll down to see, make sure you put the most important content on top. According to a usability study performed by Jakob Nielsen, many web users are reluctant to scroll beyond the first screen of information. You want to make sure that whatever the majority of users will be looking for on your site is presented at the top of the page, so that impatient users will not assume you don't have what they are looking for.

Left-Justify Your Content

Most web content should be left-justified, so the reader always has a constant location for his or her eyes to return to at the beginning of each line of text. Fully justified text is a common standard for print books; however, it is rarely used on web pages, as the ability to stretch the browser (thus reformatting the text) creates too many situations where the text is improperly spaced. Center and right justification should be reserved for special effects and used sparingly.

Highlight Important Terms

Because users will be scanning your page for information, you want them to be able to pick out important things quickly and easily. The best way to do this is to boldface (or otherwise highlight) key words or phrases. This allows users to analyze your page more quickly, as they can pick out information they need without having to read further. Keep in mind, however, that if you do highlight important information, this may be the *only* information the reader looks at, assuming that the rest is just extraneous. Also, be sure not to highlight more than five or six words in a row at most; any more, and the bold text will start to lose its stand-out effect.

EXAMPLE

You may have noticed that the previous two versions of Craig's Code Cove were overly cute in terms of headings, and that the content was not particularly well organized. We have renamed the headings and reorganized the contents of the page in Figure 3.3.

First, notice the changes in the article titles. The clever but uninformative titles "XMLalapalooza" and "Without a .Net" have been replaced with more appropriate and more descriptive titles containing key terms to which the users' eyes can be drawn. We've removed the shadow and background from the main "Articles" heading and left-justified all the headings and subheadings in order to create a nicer line down the left column.

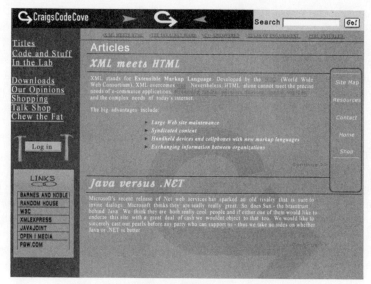

Figure 3.3 Web user interface with improved content

As for the page's macrocontent, we have shortened the text that appears for each article and provided a Continue button that will take the user to the full text. Only the most important parts of each article are shown on this page. You can find a color version of this page at CodeNotes pointer ⚙↪UI030005.

HOW AND WHY

How Much Content Should I Fit on a Single Page?

Having too much content on a single page makes it very difficult for a user to find specific information within the page. In order to make it easier for a user to find information, you should try to limit the content of each web page to a maximum of three screens (i.e., if users hit Page Down three times, they should reach the bottom of your page).

What About Searchability?

Every design suggestion is usually balanced against another facet of good design. In the case of breaking up your web content, you should always consider how your site would be searched, either internally or through an external search engine. The more pages you have for macrocontent, the less likely that a search engine will be able to properly direct a user to your site. Try to keep your content balanced with your needs for fine-grained searches. The more specific the searches, the less content you can safely distribute to multiple pages.

SUMMARY

The key fact to remember from this chapter is that writing for the Web is not the same as writing for printed media. Headings, titles, and subtitles (microcontent) will not always be seen in context on the Web, and therefore they must be far more accurate, descriptive, and well thought out. Text on the Web should come in small fragments, with one idea presented per fragment. Long texts should be broken up into multiple pages, separated by links. You need to keep in mind that web documents are not linear; you can take advantage of this fact by providing multiple paths through documents instead of simply using links to "turn the page." In order to ensure that readers recognize the important parts of your content, you should highlight key terms and phrases so that they can be immediately picked out when readers scan the page.

Topic: Navigation

Every page on your website should have some kind of navigation tools. Navigation will be most prominent, and most abundant, on your home page (the page to which most people will get by typing www.<the site>.com). Navigation needs to be easily recognizable and must tell users where they will end up if they click on a certain link.

There are six types of navigation that should be available on every website:

1. *Downward navigation.* Links that take you to subpages of the current page. For example, your home page may have a Technical Support link that takes the user to a page further into the site.
2. *Upward navigation.* Links that take you to parent pages of the current page. The home page is the only page that should not have upward navigation tools. For example, your Technical Support page should have a Home link somewhere on it that takes you back to the home page.
3. *Horizontal navigation.* Links that take you to pages that are equal to the current page in the web hierarchy. These are most often found in static menu bars with which you can move from

one part of the site to another. For example, the Technical Support page might have a link to the Contacts page, on which the users can contact the webmaster or other company staff. Both of these pages are subpages of the home page.

4. *Outward navigation.* Links that take you to pages that are outside of the domain of your website (i.e., pages other than your own). For example, a News page on your site might provide links to external websites with more information on a particular article.

5. *Forward and backward navigation.* This type of navigation should be handled by browser buttons. Backward navigation takes the user back to the previous page he or she has visited, regardless of nesting or domain. Forward navigation can occur only if backward navigation has occurred; it takes the user forward one page to where he or she has just come back from.

This topic will discuss how your pages should be organized so that navigation between them is fast and efficient.

Know Your Architecture

Before creating your website, sketch, draw site maps, or use index cards to create an organizational chart of how your site navigation will work. Know it. Test it for every scenario you can think of. Remember that there is no way that you will ever think of every possible combination of clicks that a user will perform on your site. You need to organize it so that they can find what they want without having to follow a set series of movements (although there will, of course, be patterns). In printed media, you control where your user goes next. With online media, the user controls where he or she goes, whether it be up, down, or away from your site completely.

Once you are certain that your site is easy and as foolproof as you can make it, have it running while you are designing it so that you can frequently reassess its organization.

Two Clicks

In most cases, if users must click through more than two links to get to their destination, you've lost them. One click should be your goal. Any more than two clicks, and you should have a very good reason for the complexity of your site. Examples of sites that might require more than two clicks to find something include reference sites (with multiple levels of hierarchy) and large shopping sites (although these should include searches to allow users to find things immediately).

One way of eliminating clicks is to provide an input box that will find some type of information that a user would otherwise have to search through the site for. An example of this would be the CodeNotes website, on which you can enter an eight-character CodeNotes pointer instead of having to search through lists of articles. (Of course, the option to see lists of articles is available as well.)

Menus

Menus in web pages are really just organized lists of hyperlinks, arranged in such a way that they look like an index or a table of contents. As discussed in "Page Layout," menus usually appear on the left or right sides of a page. Menus on the left are more common and are often used for more general navigation (i.e., moving between sections or levels of the website). Right-side menus are often more contextual; that is, they provide links to pages, articles, or external websites that are related to the ones you are on. This helps users who are interested in a certain aspect of your site to find other locations that might assist them as well.

Home pages of large websites will often have both right- and left-side menus, whereas pages deeper into sites sometimes eliminate the menu on the right. It is rare to find a web page with only a right-side menu.

Menus can be:

- *Static* (i.e., they always show the same options no matter where you are in a site).
- *Updating* (i.e., they show different options depending on the page you are at).
- *Collapsible* (i.e., the user can click on menu items and collapse and expand the menu to find nested links). Collapsible menus are often useful if you have a very complex site, but you do not want to present the entire navigation scheme at once.

You can find out how to create all of these types of menus using JavaScript and CSS in Chapter 8.

Navigation Bars

Navigation bars, or *navbars,* are horizontal rows of links or buttons that most often appear at the top of a web page, although there is sometimes good reason to include them at the bottom (such as navbars with Forward and Back buttons at the bottom of long pages of text). Navbars are almost always static, meaning that they appear the same on every page of your site. Your navbar should include a link to your home page, as well as links to all the major areas of your website.

Although navigation bars can be made using HTML alone, many sites choose to build their navbars out of individual images or small image maps. This can make your site much more attractive and should not add too much weight to your website as long as you keep it simple. You do not need to worry about the graphics having to reload on every page of your site, even if you are not using frames, because the user's browser should store the graphics in its cache. Simple text and graphical navigation bars, as well as rollover bars (navigation bars that highlight or darken when the user passes his or her mouse over them or clicks on them) are all detailed in Chapter 7.

One special case of navigation bar is *breadcrumbs*. Breadcrumbs are sets of links that you provide on each page of your site to give users better understanding about where they are, exactly, within your site and how to get back where they came from. For example, suppose you are running a website that sells electronic equipment. A user has navigated through your site to the description of a particular item. A set of breadcrumbs links might look like the following:

MyElectronics.com Home → Products → Microelectronics → Fantastic Plastic Machine

Each of these items would be a link back to the appropriate page. This way, instead of having to use the Back button to cycle backward through a lot of pages, users can simply follow the breadcrumbs. This is also useful when users link to a subpage of your site from a search engine or other website and want to find their way back to your home page.

Menu and Navigation Bar Positioning

Whether your main menu is at the left or on top, the accompanying subnavigation is often best placed in the other position. For example, a main menu on the left-hand side should trigger a horizontal submenu at the top of the page. Alternatively, a top horizontal main menu should have its subnavigation in the vertical left pane. There are other successful menu conventions, but these are the safest ones.

Keep menus consistent throughout your website. Don't move menus or navbars around from page to page. Don't resize menus, change fonts, or reorder menu items from page to page.

While your users should not click more than twice to find the menu item they desire, the alternative (crowding menus with countless items) is even more burdensome. Restrict menu and submenu items to eight options or less, or use a collapsible tree menu (discussed in Chapter 8) to keep too many options from appearing at once. With too many options, the page becomes crowded and confusing. Build your site architecture beforehand with this in mind.

Hyperlink Fundamentals

Link Names

The names you give to hyperlinks, whether they are menu options, navbar options, or hyperlinks embedded in text on your page, must be *descriptive*. That is, the link must tell users where it is they are going to end up if they click on it, and allow them to decide whether it is worth their time. When you are creating links within body text, make sure that the linked text is relevant. "Click here for more" is usually inadequate; "Further information on the University of Waterloo" is much more descriptive.

Similarly, with menu options, make sure you don't make them incomprehensible for the sake of brevity. Menu options will generally be shorter and less descriptive, but "Files for Download" is still better than "Really Cool Stuff!" Also, if you are going to use graphics as links, make sure that the graphic is something instantly recognizable, and that you include text along with the graphic for those who may not understand what it indicates.

Discipline your creativity when naming links. Don't use cute or funny link names. All of your links need to be clear, whether they are images or text. An image of a hammer may acceptably convey "Tools." An image of a Navajo Indian loom doesn't. A Submit button is usually fairly clear, given context. A "Give it up to da man!" button may not be.

Link Colors

Unvisited hyperlinks should *always* be blue. Although many sites find reason to change the color of unvisited links to something more appropriate to their color scheme, the only real result of this is slowing down users when they can't immediately see where all the links are on the page. Using more than one color on the same page for unvisited links, or not changing the color of the links when they become visited, is even worse; users will have no idea where they have already been.

The color of visited links tends to vary from site to site. Generally, visited links are a darker, less noticeable color than unvisited links. This does not necessarily have to be the case; what is important is that the user knows where the new information lies.

Special Cases

There are two notable special cases of types of hyperlinks that should act the same way on every site. Take care not to change how these links work, if you include them:

- Your corporate logo or your company name should *always* link back to your home page. This is an easy way for users to get back to the root of your site, without using the Back button or retyping a URL.
- People's names *should not* be `mailto` hyperlinks that automatically attempt to mail the given person if a user clicks on them. Generally, if the name of a person is a hyperlink, it should link to information on that person (just as any other hyperlink should link to information on whatever the link text is.) A hyperlink should be a `mailto` link only if it *looks* like an e-mail address (e.g., craig.wills@iscool.com).

The Back Button

The Back button is the user's safety line. It is available in every browser, and it always does the same thing: it takes the user back to the previous page he or she was on. Don't try to help the user out by designing your site so the Back button is unnecessary, works differently, or doesn't work at all. You are not helping anyone by confusing them when a button they are familiar with suddenly does something unexpected.

EXAMPLE

In this example, we optimize the Code Cove's navigation so that it will be much easier for users, and much less cluttered. The result is shown in Figure 3.4.

The original site had three different navigation bars: one on top, one on the left, and one on the right. We can make a lot more room for content and provide much better organized navigation by removing the menu on the right and incorporating it into a navbar at the top. Not only do we make the content easier to read, but we use up some of the large amount of blank space at the top of the screen. The new multilevel navbar provides three very general links (Home, Contact, and Login), and a bar of language-specific links below it. Notice that we have also changed the names of the navbar links to more subtle and more informative names.

Also take note of the fact that the unvisited links (in the first paragraph of the "XML Meets HTML" article) are now blue instead of red. Remember that blue links are easily recognizable as links by users, whereas other colors may not be. To see a full-color version of this page, go to CodeNotes pointer ⌐CNↄUI030006.

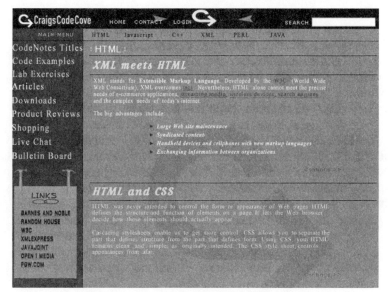

Figure 3.4   Web user interface with improved navigation

DESIGN NOTES

Button Alternatives

While browsers' standard form buttons are always a safe bet, it is un-likely that they will match your nicely designed UI. Consider using im-ages as buttons instead of the typical gray buttons. Text GIFs or icons add negligible size to your site and can improve your design tremen-dously.

Search Strategies

Searching is one of the most important and most neglected navigation tools. Not only will users often find your page through an external search engine, but once on your site, users will often go directly to the Search button to look for a particular product or particular information. Having a quick, useful, and visible search tool can provide a good safety net for users who will not use your normal navigation tools. See ᥰUI030018 for an overview of some common strategies for building search functionality into your website.

SUMMARY

The number one thing to remember about navigation is that is must be *clear and concise*. All links, buttons, and menu options should immediately indicate their destination page to users. If they do not, users may waste their time downloading pages they have no interest in and become irritated that your site's navigation is inadequate.

Make sure that every page in your site is accessible within one or two clicks. Use static menus or navigation bars to allow users to easily find their way around your site without having to search for things. Keep consistent colors for visited (always blue) and unvisited links, so that users will always know where they have been and where they haven't.

Topic: Text

Legibility can be thought of as the ease with which users can read the text on your website. The more difficult it is to read the text, the less time the users will remain on your page. Unfortunately, current screen technology prevents reading on a computer screen from being as comfortable or convenient as reading from printed media. You can, however, take steps to ensure that your website is as readable as it can possibly be, by following the guidelines provided in this topic.

Use Sans Serif Fonts for Content

Serif fonts are fonts like Times Roman or Garamond that have short lines (serifs) emanating from the upper and lower strokes of the letters. *Sans serif* fonts, like Arial and Tahoma, do not have these serifs.

Statistics show that, on the printed page, serif fonts are much easier to read than sans serif fonts. On a computer screen, the opposite is true. Due to anti-aliasing (the smoothing out of fonts done internally by most web browsers), the majority of the text on your web page should be in a sans serif font, as serif fonts become distorted at small sizes since it is difficult to create a smoothing effect with so few pixels. This includes all paragraph text, smaller headings, and menu options.

You can, however, use serif fonts for larger headings and titles, as anti-aliasing has less effect when the text is larger. Though this isn't necessary, it often provides a nice contrast with the regularity of the sans serif text on the rest of the page (just as in printed media, titles are often in sans serif fonts to contrast with the serif text).

Other font types, such as Script or Courier, should be used sparingly. Courier is often used to indicate programming language code. Script text is rarely seen on the Web, but may be used for large headers to give a page a more elegant feel.

Two of the most commonly used fonts on the Web are Tahoma (sans serif) and Times New Roman (serif). These fonts were developed by Microsoft specifically for the Web, and are much more readable than some traditional print fonts like Arial and Times Roman.

Restrict the Number of Fonts Used

Most systems will have many installed fonts which will be available in web browsers. When designing your web page, you need to exercise restraint and choose only two or three of them. If you use too many fonts, your page will look cluttered and be more difficult to read, as users will have to adjust to new fonts. Common practice is to use one font (sans serif) for all small, paragraph text, another font (serif) for headings, and possibly a third for specialty elements like boxes or call-outs. It is also often best to use default fonts that came with your system (such as the fonts that come preinstalled with Windows). Chances are, if you had to do something special to get a particular font, your users won't have it.

When selecting fonts to use, make sure you try reading a large block of text in each font to ensure that it is readable. You can find a list of commonly used fonts on the Web at CodeNotes pointer ⚭UI030007.

Contrast Text Sharply with the Background

There are many websites that are illegible because they choose font colors that are too close to the background color of the pages. Remember that black text on a white background (the color of print on paper) is the easiest to read. As you move away from these colors, your site will become less and less readable. Depending on the amount of straight text you have on your pages, it is usually acceptable to deviate somewhat from black on white—dark blue on light beige probably won't decrease readability significantly, as long as you choose an appropriate font (i.e., a sans serif font for paragraph text). Blue on red or yellow on green, however, are not acceptable combinations, because these colors are too close together in hue. Not surprisingly, white on black is almost as easy to read as black on white, although many people claim it is harder on the eyes.

Regardless of what colors you use for your font and background, you should always use *web-safe colors,* which will be discussed in the "Colors" topic section.

Use Relative Font Sizes for Content

When changing the font sizes for elements on your web page, it is often best to use relative font sizes (which are relative in size to the user's font settings, as opposed to a set point size). This ensures that you do not force font sizes that are too large or too small on your users. There are actually two steps to ensuring that your pages use relative font sizes.

1. Don't specify a basefont attribute in your <BODY> tag. This attribute indicates a default font size for the entire document. Allow users to set their own base font size in their browser preferences, and increase and decrease the font sizes on your page relative to their preference, not yours.
2. When you change the size of fonts in HTML tags or in CSS stylesheets, use relative sizes such as +2 or −1 instead of absolute sizes such as 12pt (CSS) or 4 (HTML). This way, your font sizes always increase or decrease relative to the user's preferred base font size.

Note that some modern web browsers and operating systems provide a zoom option, as opposed to simply allowing you to scale font sizes up or down with a menu option. This means that fonts (as well as everything else on the page) will be made larger relatively, regardless of whether you specified absolute or relative font sizes.

Use Emphasis Sparingly

There are many ways of emphasizing text using HTML or CSS: bold (<b>), italic (<i>), underline (<u>), color change (<font color="blue">), and the ever-more-reviled-and-less-supported blinking text (<blink>). All of these should be used sparingly on your web pages; if you use them too often, they will no longer be effective as emphasis and will make your page look patchworked.

In addition, you should try to use each type of emphasis for only a single purpose on a page. For example, if you use italics to represent text that has been quoted from another source, you should not also use it for emphasis somewhere else on the page. Readers could become confused about what you are trying to emphasize.

One special case is the use of all capital letters. Capitalized words or sentences detract from the flow of the page, because they stand out much more than any other kind of emphasis. In addition, they are difficult to read when scanning a page, as they lack the ascenders (lines and curves that stick out the top) of lowercase letters with which human readers tend to identify familiar words. Avoid using all caps if possible, especially for large blocks of text.

EXAMPLE

Craig's Code Cove, up until this point, has been very difficult to read. You would not want to read long articles (the primary purpose of this site) in the serif font that we had been using. This topic's example, shown in Figure 3.5, improves the readability of the site by changing to some much more appropriate fonts for reading on the Web.

You can see the tremendous improvement in appearance and readability a change in font makes on a web page. We've changed the header fonts and body text to Verdana, which is a sans serif font and is much easier to read on the Web. We could have used a serif font for the headings, but Verdana seemed a better choice; sans serif fonts tend to look more modern, and since this is a site for developers, modernity is a good thing.

Notice that we've also made sure that the fonts we're using contrast sharply with the background. The contrast really isn't sharp enough, however; in the example in the next topic section ("Color"), we'll completely redo the color scheme for the page, increasing readability even more. For a color version of this example, see CodeNotes pointer ⇨UI030008.

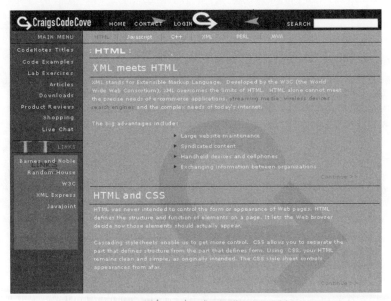

Figure 3.5   Web user interface with improved fonts

HOW AND WHY

If I Use Fonts Designed by My Company, How Can I Get Users to Use These Fonts?
In normal paragraph text on a web page, you should use only standard fonts (i.e., Times New Roman or Arial or any other fonts that are installed with your operating system). If you wish to use a different font only for headings or another very small portion of your web page, you can use images instead of text. Almost all popular graphics programs (such as Photoshop or Xara X) allow you to add special effects (such as fading from one color to another) to make your headings more distinct. However, there are a few drawbacks to using images that you should be aware of. First, the image will not be resized according to the user's settings, possibly making the font size of your heading a poor fit for the rest of the page. Second, as we will discuss in the upcoming topic, "Images," the use of images can slow down the speed at which the user can download your web page. As a final note, when using images to store text, you must make sure to follow all the rules for text presented in this topic (such as not using too many different fonts, and making sure the fonts are legible).

DESIGN NOTES

Glare Affects Legibility
Although a black-on-white color scheme is considered optimal for reading, computer screens (unlike printed pages) have the additional complication of glare. Many people find it difficult to read text on a bright white computer screen, particularly in office settings where they have no control over the lighting in the room. If you believe this will be a concern to your audience, you might consider using an off-white background color, such as `linen` (#FAF0E6), `mintcream` (#F5FFFA), or `whitesmoke` (#F5F5F5). Note that the names for these colors apply to Internet Explorer only; the hex triplets will work under any browser. Also note that these are *not* web-safe colors.

Use Absolute Font Sizes for Main Navigation
Although relative font sizes are good for ensuring that your users can always read your page comfortably, it is usually a bad idea to use relative font sizes for your main navigation tool. For example, the static button bar at the top of a page should not change size, regardless of what users do with their browsers, because you don't want it to become distorted.

Often, your menu bar will be graphical (using images as opposed to HTML text) anyway, and so will not change size dynamically. As mentioned earlier in this topic, most modern browsers have a zoom function, so that if your users truly want to increase the size of your main navigation tool, they can.

SUMMARY

The fonts you choose for your website affect how easy it will be for users to read your content and how long they will want to keep reading. You should minimize the number of fonts you use on a single web page, and make sure that you are using a sans serif font for all body text you expect users to read easily. You can use serif fonts for headers and subheaders, because larger font sizes are not affected as much by antialiasing (smoothing out fonts). When emphasizing certain text, be sure to use bold or italics (instead of capital letters), and use them consistently. Try to use relative font sizes as much as possible to avoid overriding the font size settings that users have set in their browsers.

Topic: Colors

A website's color scheme can make or break it. People will often perceive the quality, complexity, and mood of a website simply by what colors it uses. If people are repulsed by the colors you have chosen for your pages, there is a good chance they will go somewhere else without ever having read any of your content.

Color choice can be extremely subtle, but can have a large impact on the effectiveness of your site. Most people who are not experienced designers have difficulty selecting colors that look good together and that provide the mood they want for their website. This chapter will give you some quick insights into how to choose appropriate colors, and provides a few simple ideas on how to find a scheme that works for you.

CONCEPTS

RGB

RGB (which stands for "red, green, blue") is a *color space*. That is, it is a set of primary colors from which all other colors can be created. The three colors in this color space represent the three colors of light to which the human eye is sensitive. By adding different amounts of these three primaries together, any color in the visible spectrum can be created.

Colors can be represented in HTML using RGB hex triplets. Each of these contains three 2-digit hexadecimal numbers, which represent the amount of red, green, and blue in a color. For example, the word "Alert!" in the following HTML snippet is red (the primary color) because its red value is set to FF and its other two values are 00.

```
<font color="#FF0000">Alert!</font>
```

An absence of all three primary colors creates black (hex triplet #000000). Maximum values for all three colors creates white (hex triplet #FFFFFF). Using this notation, you can conceivably create 2^{24} different colors. However, most browsers (and many monitors) do not support this full color range. In fact, there are only 216 web-safe colors (discussed in a later section) that are guaranteed to appear the same on every browser. For now, you should remember that an arbitrary color choice on your computer might not look the same on a different computer.

Terminology

There are a few color theory terms you should know and understand before continuing with the rest of this chapter.

Hue

Hue is almost a synonym for color. A color's hue is what gives it its name. For example, objects (or web page elements) can be of orange hue, turquoise hue, or any other named or unnamed hue.

Saturation

The saturation of an object is how intense its color is. The more colorful an object, the more highly saturated it is. Lower saturation results in darker, more neutral colors. When you are using hexadecimal triplets to represent colors in your HTML, you are, in effect, selecting the saturation of red, green, and blue that appears in each color.

Brightness

In reality, brightness is the amount of light reflected by a particular color. The more light a color reflects, the brighter it appears to the human eye. Colors available for web page design have varying levels of brightness depending on the hex triplets you use to select the color.

Contrast

The contrast of the colors on a page is the difference between them. Bright colors seem brighter when they are next to, or on top of, darker colors. High-contrast color schemes (such as bright yellow and dark blue) are not recommended, as they are hard on the eyes, distracting, and somewhat unprofessional.

The Color Wheel

Before we talk about color schemes, we will introduce you to the color wheel. A color wheel represents the spectrum of available colors in such a way that you can immediately see the relationships between them. We'll talk more about these relationships in the next section. For now, have a look at the color wheel at CodeNotes pointer ⊶**CN**⟩UI030009.

Color Schemes

Before designing your website, you should come up with a color scheme that you will use. What colors you choose may depend on the type of site you are creating (hot colors, cold colors), the attitude of your site (bright colors or dark colors), or even your company's corporate color scheme (in which case you may have less control than you wish over what colors you use for your website). Obviously, this chapter cannot cover every attractive and semiattractive color scheme available. There will always be exceptions to rules, or room for slight adjustments here and there. The following are some suggested guidelines for selecting a color scheme to suit your website; these guidelines may be bent or broken as you see fit. Keep in mind, however, that there are reasons for the selections in each one, and that the further you stray from them the more chance there is that your site will clash or become unattractive to some people.

Complementary

Complementary colors are colors that appear directly across from one another in the color wheel. For example, in the color wheel shown at CodeNotes pointer ⊶**CN**⟩UI030009, lime green and dark violet are complementary colors. Complementary colors tend to look good together, and many websites choose their color schemes by first selecting one color and then finding its complement on the color wheel.

Keep in mind, however, that most complementary colors should not be mixed in equal portions. It is usually better to use more of the darker of the two colors and less of the brighter one. Table 3.1 will help you decide how much of each complementary color to use.

Complementary Colors	Ratio
Red/Green	1:1 (50% green, 50% red)
Blue/Orange	5:3 (~65% blue, ~35% orange)
Violet/Yellow	6:1 (~85% violet, 15% yellow)

Table 3.1   Complementary color ratios

Colors close to those presented in Table 3.1 will also work in similar ratios (i.e., lighter blue with lighter orange). Keep in mind that using a complementary color scheme does not restrict you to two colors; more complex color wheels show many slight variations on each hue that you can choose from and still have a relatively attractive page.

One problem with complementary color schemes is that they can look unprofessional if they are used at full saturation. This is because computer screens tend to make colors look brighter than they would on paper. However, sites like Amazon.com make complementary color schemes (blue and yellow in Amazon's case) look good by desaturating the colors, so that they share enough gray to be compatible. Most likely, the only time you will want to use complementary colors at full saturation is if you are creating a header or small graphic that needs to stand out.

Also remember that your color scheme should not involve breaking other rules of good web page design, such as readability. Most of the time, you should still be using black text, and white or light-colored backgrounds for large blocks of text.

Analogous
Analogous color schemes are produced by selecting a series of colors that occur next to each other on the color wheel (and therefore are related in saturation). For example, in the color wheel at CodeNotes pointer ⌀CNUI030009, we could choose to use the three colors that appear in the bottom right quarter of the wheel (ranging from orange to yellow). The rules for color ratios are similar to those mentioned in Table 3.1: try to mix more of a darker color with less of a brighter one. With the orange and yellow example, you would probably want to use slightly more orange than bright yellow.

Analogous color schemes are often used to convey a website's mood. Generally, you can tell what mood your color scheme will produce by looking at where those colors appear in nature, and how human beings react to natural occurrences of those colors. For example, the yellow to red section of the color wheel is often called the "warm" or "hot" colors, as these colors occur most commonly in fire. Hot colors, with the addition of black, tend to provide an exciting, urgent, or modern mood to a web page. Alternatively, the green to violet section of the spectrum (the "cool" or "cold" colors) portray calmness, professionalism, or elegance. Cold colors, with the addition of white, are often associated with flora, water, and snow.

Remember that color schemes do not always have to be natural. It is perfectly possible, for example, to create an urban or technological mood for your site using a mixture of low-saturation cold colors (blues and violets) and grays.

Monochromatic
Sometimes you can create an extremely attractive website using only one color (or two saturations of the same color) combined with black and white. A very popular combination on many modern websites is a dark red or blue with black and white. Monochromatic color schemes can be created simply by selecting a "pie slice" in the color wheel. You can use variations in saturation to provide a little variety (e.g., by changing the saturation of the dark blue to a light blue).

Monochromatic color schemes tend to convey less ambiance than other color schemes, but still can be used to create a very modern appearance on a web page. In fact, monochromatic schemes are probably one of the most popular design palettes used today, both online and offline. This is because they are easier on the eyes than other color schemes (as there is no chance of clashing colors), and because it is more difficult to associate another organization's color scheme with a monochromatic website.

Color Symbolism
North Americans tend to have some preconceived perceptions of the meanings of different colors. The following list of color connotations is quoted from an article on CNet.com (Carrie Gatlin, *Secrets of Web Color Revealed*, http://builder.cnet.com/webbuilding/0-3883-8-6309338-5.html). When choosing a color scheme for your website, keep this list in mind, as it may affect how your site is perceived:

- *Red.* Passion, romance, fire, violence, aggression, stop or warning.
- *Purple.* Creativity, mystery, royalty, mysticism, rarity.
- *Blue.* Loyalty, security, conservatism, tranquility, coldness, sadness.
- *Green.* Nature, fertility, growth, envy, money.
- *Yellow.* Brightness, illumination, illness, cowardice.

- **Black.** Power, sophistication, contemporary style, death, morbidity, evil.
- **White.** Purity, innocence, cleanliness, truth, peace, coldness, sterility.

Web-Safe Colors

Web-safe colors are a set of 216 colors that are compatible across multiple platforms for people with low-end (256-color) monitors. These colors were selected mathematically rather than aesthetically, and the set of available colors has dissatisfied many professional designers. Nevertheless, if you want to ensure that your web pages will appear in the same colors for all your users, regardless of browser or platform, you need to make use of only web-safe colors.

The web-safe palette is made up of colors that have 0 percent, 20 percent, 40 percent, 60 percent, 80 percent, or 100 percent of each of red, green, or blue. For example, #FFCC33 and #003399 are web-safe colors, whereas #DDCC33 and #12CDAB are not because they contain hexadecimal numbers that are not in the given saturation percentages. Colors that are not web-safe will look different depending on whether you view them in Internet Explorer, or Netscape, or on a PC or a Macintosh.

Generally, you should worry about web-safe colors only if you are truly aiming your website toward the lowest common denominator. You can find a web-safe color palette at CodeNotes pointer ⟳UI030010.

EXAMPLE

This example introduces some major changes to the website. Take a look at Figure 3.6.

We have chosen an analogous color scheme for this website; orange and red are next to each other on the color wheel. We have made the background an off-white color, and made the text black. The readability of the content section of this page is now nearly optimal. The black on yellow is not quite so easy to read, but we have used this combination only for short menu options and not for blocks of text, so readability is not as important. The new color scheme is far less eye-straining than the old. To see a color version of this example, go to CodeNotes pointer ⟳UI030011. In the next topic, we will put the finishing touches on the new-and-improved Craig's Code Cove.

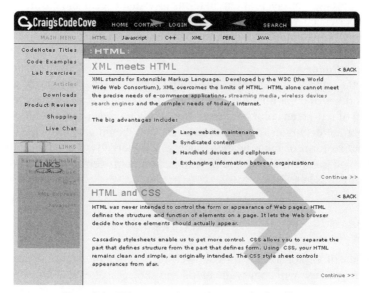

Figure 3.6   Web user interface with improved color scheme

HOW AND WHY

What Do I Do If My Corporate Colors Do Not Lend Themselves to an Attractive Color Scheme?

If you find that your corporate colors do not fit easily with any of the color strategies we have discussed in this topic, you can cheat by using colors that are close to your corporate colors but still fit with the color scheme. Also, if you find that some of your corporate colors fit into a color scheme, but one or two do not (for example, if your corporate colors are blue, orange, and green), you can minimize the use of the non-matching color, and desaturate it as much as possible, to decrease the effect of the odd color.

BUGS AND CAVEATS

Use Blue Text for Links Only

One caveat to applying a color scheme involves hyperlinks. Because the recognized (and default) color for hyperlinks is blue, it is usually best not to change this. Regardless of the color scheme you are using for the rest of your site, your hyperlinks should still be blue. This usually does not present a serious problem in terms of visual appeal and ensures that inexperienced web users, or even experienced web users who are not paying full attention, always know where they can click.

Color Blindness

Another significant caveat to designing your color scheme is to consider the effects of color blindness. Roughly 1 in 10 males is affected by some form of red-green color blindness. If you rely on red and green colors as important distinguishing characteristics, you should also provide an alternative form of identification, such as a differently-shaped icon. For more on color blindness and how to design your website around color blindness, see ∘^{CN}UI030019.

SUMMARY

Choice of a color scheme for your website is extremely important, as the colors you use will convey the mood and subject matter of your website before the user even gets to the textual content. Though there are many different possibilities for colors you can use, it is best to stay close to one of several color scheme options: complementary (colors opposite one another on the color wheel), graduating (colors next to one another on the color wheel), or monochromatic (variations on colors in a single pie slice of the color wheel). Remember that if you are designing for a large audience who may be using older computers, it is always best to use the web-safe color palette that will be compatible across multiple browsers and platforms.

Topic: Images

Almost every website will need more than just text to get its point across. Graphics and photographs can often convey information much more clearly than simple text. HTML makes it quite simple to include icons, diagrams, photographs, and background images on your Web pages.

However, images have some serious drawbacks. They can clutter a web page, and downloading pages with images in them takes much longer than downloading text-only pages. This is not to say that you should avoid using images. This chapter will provide you with some helpful tips on how to use images effectively and minimize unnecessary use of images to avoid long download times and poorly rendered sites.

CONCEPTS

Arranging Your Site around Images

When surfing the Web, it is very irritating to arrive at a site that unexpectedly takes 30, 60, or more seconds before it finishes loading. With a little rearrangement, you can ensure that your site will not cause people to hit the Back button before it even finishes loading.

Don't Put Large Images on the Main Page

Large photographs or diagrams on the main page of your site will always cause problems, particularly if your site has high traffic or your users have low bandwidth. One or two smaller images are fine; you might use one for your corporate logo and one in the text of the page for something important. You might even want to use some small images instead of HTML for your navigation tools. This is OK. What you should avoid are long lists of big images, introductory screens with huge photographs (you should avoid introductory screens anyway), or detailed image maps. If you want your user to find something quickly, make sure your page will load quickly.

Avoid Big Background Images

Background images can make your site look great; however, they can also slow it down to a crawl. It is usually best to avoid background images unless you can be sure that your user base is mostly high-bandwidth or that they don't mind the wait time. If you really want to use a background image, make sure you have saved it with a simple color scheme (such as 16 colors) and lower image quality than you would normally use (increase the compression). This will result in a fuzzy or undetailed image, but you should not need detail for background images.

Use Reduced-Size Thumbnails

If you want to show images on your main page, use reduced-size thumbnails and link them to the large images. When creating thumbnails, it is usually better to crop the most relevant part of the image, rather than trying to shrink the whole thing down into a smaller space. Changing the size of images usually makes them lose quality. If you have a picture of a person, create a thumbnail of his or her face, which, when clicked on, will display the full image including the upper body. Remember to always make sure your thumbnails have context (i.e., some kind of text underneath them) so that users know what they are clicking on. Also, like any image, thumbnails should have <alt> tags so that if the graphics do not load for some reason, users will still know what the link is for.

Warn Your Users

In addition to providing them with thumbnails and context for those thumbnails, users will always appreciate it if you warn them when they will be downloading a large image file. For example, you could have a small thumbnail image of a product you are selling, with the text underneath it reading "Bob's Fantastic Potato Chip Maker (JPEG, 523K)." This way, users know they are going to be downloading a larger-than-average graphic and can choose whether it is really worth their while to do so.

Use <ALT> Tags for All Images

HTML allows you to specify text that will appear in place of an image. Not only does this provide an alternative for visually challenged users or users with graphics turned off, but it also allows users to see what images will be before the page finishes loading or if there is a problem finding some of the images. You can specify alternative text for an image like this:

```
<img src="images/chipmaker.jpeg" alt="Bob's Fantastic Potato
Chip Maker">
```

Keep in mind that alternate text may not display correctly unless you explicitly specify the size of your image, as explained in the next section.

Specify Image Sizes

You should include sizes in your HTML (height and width) for every image you include on your web pages. The image size you specify in your HTML should be exactly the same as the actual size of the image. Do not use the height and width attributes to enlarge or shrink images; you will lose quality and distort the image. The following HTML shows you how to specify an image size:

```
<img src="images/sushi.jpg" width="75" height="50" alt="Seven-
piece sushi plate with California rolls">
```

There are two reasons for specifying image size:

1. Since browsers render the HTML first and the images second, they will be able to assign appropriate spacing for images before they are actually downloaded. This ensures that the page layout is correct from the beginning, so that the browser does

not render the page as though the images had no size, and then have to render it again once it downloads the images.

2. <alt> tags, as discussed in the previous section, will be displayed correctly. If the images have no size attributes, and for some reason do not display correctly (or are taking a long time to load), you will not be able to see the alternate text, as the image box will be too tiny to display it.

Always specify height and width for every image, to avoid complications when your site is loading.

Note that using the height and width attributes to shrink images will not decrease download size. The user's browser still has to download and decompress the image at full size, and then resize it in his or her window. Thus, you are actually slowing things down for the user by forcing a resize. Specify only those height and width attributes that match the real size of the file. If you want to resize your graphics, do it in a graphics program like Photoshop or Xara X.

GIFs and JPEGs

GIF and JPEG are the two types of image files that are viewable in browsers. Most graphics programs (such as Adobe Photoshop, Corel-Draw!, or Xara X) will export files in GIF or JPEG format. Each of these formats has its advantages. It is usually fairly easy to determine whether you should use the GIF or JPEG format on your website, if you stick to the following simple rules.

GIFs

Use GIF for diagrams, computer-generated graphics, images with a lot of solid color, and images that contain text. GIF (which stands for Graphics Interchange Format), originally a CompuServ (since acquired by Unisys) proprietary format, uses a compression scheme called LZW (Lempel-Zev-Welch). Some graphics applications may not be able to create GIFs, as any application that uses the the LZW scheme must obtain a license from Unisys.

GIF is a lossless compression format and generally results in images that are two to five times larger than JPEG for the same pixel resolution. However, where JPEGs may lose colors during compression, GIFs preserve every pixel value and are therefore superior if you need precise color details in your graphics. GIF, when used for graphics with large fields of color, may actually be smaller that JPEG, because of the way in which LZW compression works. (See CodeNotes pointer ⌐ᴺUI030012 for a simple explanation of the LZW compression algorithm.)

When saving GIFs, you should optimize them using an *adaptive* color palette (sometimes called a *nearest color* palette). This palette derives image colors from your image instead of from a preset system or browser color palette, and will look better on 24-bit browser displays.

JPEGs

Use JPEG for photographs. Although JPEG (which stands for Joint Photographic Experts Group) uses *lossy* compression algorithms (meaning that some information may be lost during compression), photographs are usually complex enough that the human eye does not notice the loss in quality. JPEG files are much smaller than GIFs when used for photographs and will almost invariably look better because of the dithering effects on GIFs. Many graphics applications will permit you to choose the quality of your JPEG images, allowing you to create lower-quality (and therefore smaller-size) images; in most web browsers, you can sacrifice a great deal of quality before you notice a real difference in the appearance of your graphics.

For both formats (GIF and JPEG), smaller color palettes and lower quality result in smaller files. Keep in mind that graphics will be *dithered* into web-safe palettes on most people's browsers; that is, colors that the browser does not support will be replaced with the browser's closest alternative color.

Tiling Background Images

Tiling background images offer the advantage of taking one small image and allowing the browser to repeat it continuously horizontally and vertically, creating a patterned background for your web page. The file size of the image remains small, and it allows infinite design possibilities for your background. However, in most cases, tiling backgrounds impair readability and look poor. Many designers would argue that they are an indicator of amateur web page design. If you do use a background tile, be sure that it is extremely light in saturation and not busy. Your best bet, though, is not to use tiling background images at all.

EXAMPLE

The example in this topic is the final version of the Craig's Code Cove website, shown in Figure 3.7.

We've removed all of the extraneous images (the extra logo in the title bar, the background image behind the text, and the image in the title of the Links menu, in order to make the page load faster. The dark text on pale background is now optimally readable, and the page will load quickly even for users with low bandwidth. The only image still being used is the Craig's Code Cove logo at the top left corner of the screen. This logo, which, of course, appears on every page in the website, is a link back to the Craig's Code Cove home page.

You can see a color version of this example at CodeNotes pointer UI030013. You can also find full HTML and CSS code for this final version of the Craig's Code Cove page at CodeNotes pointer UI030014.

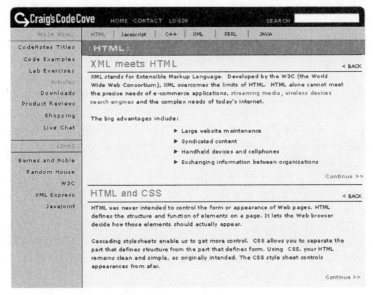

Figure 3.7   Web user interface with improved images

BUGS AND CAVEATS

Avoid Banner-Shaped Images
The sad truth is that the overwhelming number of banner ads appearing on the Web in the last few years has caused most Web users to start tuning out anything shaped remotely like a banner advertisement. Although you may occasionally want graphics or boxes in the shape of skinny, horizontal bars, you should try to avoid this shape if the content of those elements is important, because there is a good chance that users will simply ignore them.

Avoid Time-Wasters

You should avoid putting on your website anything that will needlessly keep your users from getting where they want to go. Many of these are image related. Major time-wasters include:

- Graphical Welcome screens for your website that require the user to click through them to get to the main pages.
- Large or complicated background images or image maps that take a long time to load on slow connections.
- Distractions such as animated GIFs, scrolling text windows, or flashing text. Generally, anything that requires that the user do more work or wait longer to get to the meat of your site should be kept to a minimum or avoided entirely.

SUMMARY

Too many images, very large images, or poorly optimized images can make wait times for pages far too long. Yet when optimized and chosen intelligently, images enhance your site, with the side effect of a little extra download time.

A good target to aim for is having the main page of your site (to which the most people link directly) be under 75K in size. This is usually enough space for two to three small images, and a page or two of HTML text. If your page is any larger than this, the wait time for the page to load will start to become noticeable. Pages that are deeper into your site can be larger in size—very large, as long as you warn users before they click on the link.

You can optimize your main page for all users by providing thumbnails that link to larger images, providing exact sizes in your HTML for the widths and heights of images, and providing alternative text that your users can see before the images have actually loaded (or if something goes wrong). Be sure to choose the correct image format: GIF for diagrams and text, and JPEG for photographs.

Remember that, compared to images, HTML colors, text, and tables add minimal weight to the file size of your page, and thus are preferable to images and other enhancements whenever possible.

Topic: Technology Constraints

There are many great technologies available to enhance websites beyond the capabilities of static HTML. We discuss some of the more commonly supported ones in this CodeNote: JavaScript, DHTML, and XML/XSLT. Other technologies that add to the appearance or usability of a website include Flash (used for creating non-HTML-based graphical/animated websites or web pages, often with sound) and Shockwave (used for web entertainment; things like games, animated movies, and web greeting cards). All of these technologies are already or are becoming supported by a large percentage of the Internet community. However, when deciding whether to use them, you must consider how much of your potential user base you are willing to alienate by using a new or nonstandard technology, and whether it is worth it.

CONCEPTS

Targeting Your Users

You know what kind of service you want your website or web application to provide, but you need to decide who your users will be. The type of site you are creating will determine the number and complexity of additional technologies you should use in its creation.

For example, if your site is geared toward developers, you are most likely safe using technologies such as JavaScript, DHTML, and XML, because most developers will be using the most up-to-date browsers that support all of these tools. You probably don't want to use Flash or Shockwave, however, because the developers will not want to waste time with animation and graphics in order to get to the details.

If, on the other hand, your site is intended to be for a more general audience, you have more choices to make. If your site deals with entertainment, such as games or movies, you may want to include some Flash on your pages to make them more exciting; keep in mind, however, that your users will need to download additional applications (if they haven't already) in order for your site to work correctly. This is often a serious deterrent to those users who are on slow connections and don't have these technologies; be certain that you only want users who will be willing to download to use your site.

If you're trying to gear your site toward the majority, many of the cool web technologies like Flash or Shockwave are probably bad ideas. Websites such as online stores or informational websites not geared toward tech-industry audiences are probably best created using older, less bandwidth-intensive technologies.

Covering the Lowest Common Denominator — Or Not
According to Jakob Nielsen, the only technology you are truly safe with is HTML 1.0. Anything beyond that and you start to cut users out of your potential audience.

Obviously, no one today designs websites using the HTML 1.0 standard, the original HTML from the early 1990s (HTML 4.01 is the latest HTML recommendation, released in late 1999). Even HTML 2.0 is considered obsolete by the W3C. At some point, you have to accept that you are going to lose a few customers and design your website for the majority. What you have to decide, however, is where to stop.

As a general rule, it is best not to design your website using technologies or features available only in the newest browsers. For example, if you were to design a website at the time of this writing, you would not want to take advantage of features found only in Netscape 6 or Internet Explorer 6, unless you could be sure that most of your user base would be using these browsers. If you want to maintain a large audience for your site, you would be relatively safe designing for Netscape 4 and above, or Internet Explorer 5 and above. To play it really safe, design for third-generation (version 3) browsers. At the time of this writing, anything earlier is probably not worth your while, because very few people are still using earlier browsers.

In short, it is up to you to decide where to draw the line. The further back the technology you support, the more users you accommodate, but at some point the convenience of new technologies outweighs the importance of making everyone happy. See the appendix at the end of this CodeNote for a helpful timeline that shows what technologies (versions of JavaScript, DHTML support, etc.) were introduced in each version of the major browsers.

Questionable Technologies
Some technologies acquire bad reputations because when they are first introduced, they are buggy and slow. Many web designers continue to shun new technologies like Flash, Shockwave, and even frames (which were introduced by Netscape as an additional technology and then implemented in HTML 4.0) simply because they have had bad experiences with them. This is partially justified: all of these technologies do indeed have some severe drawbacks and inherently break many of the features of good web page design, such as bookmarking (frames), the Back button (Flash), and optimal wait time (Flash, Shockwave, etc.).

However, all of these questionable technologies can be used correctly, and with restraint, to improve the usability and presentation of your website. Once you know who your users are, you can decide whether it is worthwhile having them download Flash, or whether they will appreciate a frames layout. Remember: It is not the technologies that are bad, it is the way in which they are implemented.

XML and XSLT

Extensible Markup Language (XML) is similar to HTML except that it does not have a specific set of tag names; instead, XML allows you to define your own tag names. XML can be used to represent any kind of structured data in a universal text format. XML Stylesheet Language Transforms (XSLT) is a language for transforming XML data into HTML (or, really, any other text-based format). If you are designing a web page that includes content extracted from a database into XML format, you can use XSLT to format it for display on your website. One major advantage of XSLT is that you can create a variety of scripts, each of which will transform your XML into a web page compatible with a different browser (i.e., you could have one that transforms your XML into an Internet Explorer–compatible web page and one that transforms your XML into a Netscape-compatible web page). XML and XSLT, as well as methods for leveraging them on your website, are discussed in Chapter 6 of this CodeNote.

SUMMARY

It is always best not to support only the "latest and greatest" technologies, in terms of browsers and browser plug-ins. Although you can certainly take advantage of a new feature where it is available, you should always make sure that it will not break, look strange, or cause errors in older browsers. By knowing the type of people who make up your user base, you can decide just how far back are the versions you need to support, and whether it is worthwhile to incorporate nonstandard technologies into your web page designs. When in doubt, however, always cater to the lowest common denominator.

Chapter Summary

The appearance and usability of web user interfaces can be greatly improved by adhering to a few simple rules and principles. In brief summation, these rules are:

- **Page Layout** Content should take up around 80 percent of your screen; the remaining 20 percent should be used for navigation tools or headers (or advertisements, if necessary). Choose the lowest resolution for which you want to design your page, and design for that resolution and higher. Try to be resolution-independent wherever possible, so that users who are not using standard window sizes will still be able to view your page correctly.
- **Content** All of your page titles, headings, and subheadings (microcontent) should be clear and descriptive. You want users to know exactly what they are looking at. Always try to avoid cute or clever microcontent. The rest of the content on your page (macrocontent) should be broken up into page-sized chunks wherever possible. Remember to put the most important content at the top of your page, because people don't like to scroll. Try to highlight important terms in your content, so users who are scanning the page can pick things out.
- **Navigation** Your navigation should usually be on the top and left of your page. Make sure all of the links on your menus and navbars are clear, and that they tell users exactly where they are going to end up. Unvisited hyperlinks should always be blue, because this is a web-wide norm. When designing your navigation scheme, try to be sure that users can get anywhere they want to go within one or two clicks.
- **Text** Use a sans serif font (like Verdana) for body text. If you want, you can use a serif font (like Georgia) for headings and subheadings, as serif fonts look fine at larger sizes on the Web. All of your text should contrast sharply with the background; as soon as you vary from black on white, readability starts to decrease. Restrict the number of fonts used on your page to two or three, and use emphasis sparingly.
- **Colors** If possible, you should use the 216 web-safe colors when designing for the Web. Select a color scheme for your website that uses only one or two colors, and variations on the saturation and brightness of those colors. Use the color wheel to determine what colors go well together. Sample color schemes include complementary (colors opposite each other on the color wheel), associative (colors next to each other on the color wheel), and monochrome (a single color on the color wheel, plus black and white).
- **Images** Use images sparingly, as they add a great deal of weight to web pages and significantly increase download times. Minimize images on your home page, and use thumbnails that

link to larger images instead. Always provide users with a size for the image they will be downloading, so that they can determine whether it is worth it with their bandwidth. Use <alt> tags for all of your images, and specify width and height for each image so that the browser does not have to rerender the page after downloading the images. For image formats, use JPEG for photographs and GIF for everything else.

When designing your user interface, always keep in mind the technologies that your users will be working with. You can't always design for everyone, but you can cater to a much wider audience by not forcing them to download and use bandwidth-intensive or nonstandard technologies. The following chapters illustrate many different technologies that you can use to apply these rules.

Chapter 4

—

JAVASCRIPT

At first glance, JavaScript will seem familiar to any developer proficient in a third-generation language such as C, C++, Java, or Perl. While JavaScript is designed to be limited in its interaction with an underlying Operating System (it is not allowed to effect changes beyond the browser, it can't write files, etc.), it is, nonetheless, a complete language featuring traditional constructs such as variables, functions, and objects. Upon closer inspection, you will find that there are a few architectural peculiarities to the language, such as prototype-based inheritance. For the most part, however, JavaScript is straightforward and easy to learn for anyone who is comfortable programming in another complex language.

Before exploring the details of the language, it is important to eliminate a few misconceptions concerning JavaScript. First of all, JavaScript has no relationship to Java; it is not a derivative of Java, it is missing many of Java's features, and it is not bound in any way to the Java language specification. Furthermore, the "Script" in JavaScript often gives the impression that JavaScript is a weak language, suited only to writing small, simple scripts and macros. While JavaScript cannot, for security reasons, write or read files on a hard drive or call operating system APIs, it is a significant language supporting almost every feature (objects, inheritance, variables, functions, arrays, etc.) one would expect from a nonscripting language. Later in this chapter, you will read a brief section on the history of JavaScript, which will provide more insight into how these diminished opinions of JavaScript came about.

JavaScript is incredibly useful for web-based user interfaces in that it provides a fairly simple mechanism for making a web page react to user actions. Because JavaScript is built into the web page and is executed by the user's browser, it is very fast and responsive. Simple JavaScript additions to a web page can perform basic data-field validation, highlight critical information, and even change content based on user input. Used appropriately, JavaScript can dramatically improve the usability of a web-based user interface.

SIMPLE APPLICATION

Listing 4.1 illustrates a very simple web page with JavaScript content:

```
<HTML>
  <SCRIPT language="JavaScript">
  <!--
    // alert() is a built-in JavaScript function
    alert("Simple Example");
  //-->
  </SCRIPT>
</HTML>
```

Listing 4.1   Simple.html

Save Listing 4.1 as Simple.html and load Simple.html in your browser. An alert box will be displayed on the screen with the contents "Simple Example."

CORE CONCEPTS

Browsers and JavaScript
JavaScript is most commonly used to create interactive web pages. JavaScript appears on an HTML page between two special tags: <SCRIPT> and </SCRIPT>. The browser receives JavaScript as part of a web page and will automatically run the code as appropriate. In most cases, JavaScript code will be run by a browser as a response to some form of event. For example, you will notice that menu items on web pages will often change color or shading as you move the mouse over them. This is simply a bit of JavaScript that was associated by the web page author with the browser's pre-defined onMouseOver event, as illustrated in Listing 4.2

```
<HTML>
  <SCRIPT language="JavaScript">
    function makeRed(e) {e.srcElement.style.color="#FF0000" }
    function makeGreen(e) {e.srcElement.style.color="#00FF00"}
  </SCRIPT>
  <p onmouseover="makeRed(event)"
     onmouseout="makeGreen(event)">hello</p>
</HTML>
```

Listing 4.2   The onMouseOver event

We will discuss events in the "Event Handlers" topic of Chapter 5. However, this example does illustrate just how easy it can be to use JavaScript to respond to browser events. JavaScript can also be used to manipulate the browser itself, opening new windows, moving backward and forward through browser history, popping up alert messages, and performing other tasks. JavaScript can also make dynamic changes to the HTML in a web page via the Document Object Model (DOM) supported by all major browsers and covered in the "Document Object Model" topic in Chapter 5.

This chapter focuses primarily on the basic features of JavaScript, such as creating script blocks and functions. The second topic in this chapter discusses using JavaScript to execute regular expressions on text.

JavaScript History

JavaScript, a creation of Sun Microsystems, was originally called Live-Script, but was later renamed for marketing reasons. Predictably, Netscape and Microsoft browsers originally implemented slightly different versions of the language. As an added complication, JavaScript was supported through a Document Object Model (DOM) that is proprietary to each browser. Not only would different browsers offer different JavaScript features, the proprietary DOMs allowed a situation where supported JavaScript behaved differently on different browsers.

In 1997, with the help of the European Computer Manufacturers Association (ECMA), JavaScript was unambiguously defined in a public specification known as ECMAScript. Versions 4 and above of both Netscape and Microsoft browsers implement the ECMAScript standard and are compatible, at least in terms of the core JavaScript language. New versions of Internet Explorer add a few nonstandard features to provide backward compatibility with the previous Document Object Model. Netscape 6's implementation, however, is not backward-compatible with earlier Netscape DOMs, much to the chagrin of developers with Netscape 4–compatible websites. This CodeNote will explore only those features common to both browsers and will specifically identify features that differ when the need arises.

The second problem of different DOM implementations was not resolved until recently, when both IE 6 and Netscape 6 adopted the standard DOM supported by the World Wide Web Consortium (W3C). With the combination of a standard JavaScript language (ECMAScript), and the standardized Document Object Model, many compatibility issues have finally been resolved. However, not every user will be working with IE 6 or Netscape 6, so you have to keep this history in mind as you work out JavaScript compatibility issues.

Assumptions for This Chapter

This chapter is intended to introduce a developer who is comfortable developing in at least one other language with the core aspects of JavaScript. It is not a complete reference, and, as such, some details and features of the language are not presented here. This chapter will, however, give you enough orientation to be able to understand and develop in JavaScript in the context of creating interactive web pages. See the CodeNotes website for a list of additional JavaScript references ⟳**CN**⟳UI040001.

Topic: JavaScript Language Basics

If you are familiar with Java, C, or C++, you should not have any problems with JavaScript's syntax. The JavaScript syntax conventions are common ones: code blocks are denoted by curly braces, variables are declared using a keyword followed by a variable name, and all statements should end with a semicolon (although in JavaScript the semicolons are technically optional). There is certainly more to it, however. JavaScript is subtly different from other languages in ways that may seem unusual at first, but are ultimately easy to understand. This topic explores the basic syntax of JavaScript and illustrates some common uses. Many advanced JavaScript features, such as event handling, are covered in Chapter 5.

CONCEPTS

JavaScript in HTML Documents

To put JavaScript in an HTML document, you need only place your code between `<SCRIPT language="JavaScript">` and `</SCRIPT>` tags.

If you want to run your script only if the browser supports a particular version of JavaScript (such as 1.3, supported by IE 5 and Netscape 6), you can use the language attribute to specify this, as shown in Listing 4.3.

```
<SCRIPT language="JavaScript1.3">
<!--
/* code goes here
...
*/
//-->
</SCRIPT>
```

Listing 4.3   Specifying a particular version of JavaScript

In any case, if the language attribute is not included in the <script> element, most browsers will simply default to the latest version of JavaScript. There was once a time when Microsoft's VBScript was a rival to JavaScript; however, VBScript only runs on Internet Explorer and is being abandoned by Microsoft, so its use is discouraged.

One other note about Listing 4.3: JavaScript code is conventionally placed between <!-- and --> tags. <!-- and --> are the opening and closing tags for HTML comments. JavaScript code between HTML comments will be ignored by browsers that do not support JavaScript. If you omit the comment tags, an older browser might parse the JavaScript as if it were ordinary HTML text.

JavaScript supports C- and C++ style comment markup such as // (for one-line comments) and /* */ (for comments that span multiple lines). You should always place a // before the closing HTML comment tag (-->) that you have used to encompass your script, so that the browser will not try to interpret it as JavaScript code. In other words, the JavaScript interpreter will ignore <!--, but will consider --> a syntax error.

Last, you should keep in mind as we progress through the examples that JavaScript is case-sensitive for both reserved words and variable names.

Data Types and Variables

JavaScript is a loosely typed language. In other words, it doesn't have distinct data types for its variables. In many languages, you declare your variables by specifying a data type for the variable, and then a name (e.g., int myInteger). In JavaScript, myInteger would simply be declared using the var keyword. JavaScript variables can hold any data type, at any time. For example, examine Listing 4.4:

```
<SCRIPT>
<!--
  var x;
  x=3;
  x="Hi there";
  x=3.14;
  x=true;
//-->
</SCRIPT>
```

Listing 4.4   Declaring and assigning values to a variable

In Listing 4.4, note that the third line, var x, is good form, but optional. The variable x is not actually created until some value is assigned to it. As you can see from the following lines, the value could be any data type, and it could be assigned at any time. Explicitly declaring your variables is necessary, however, if you wish to declare a local variable inside a function when the variable will have the same name as a global variable.

Primitives and Objects
While there is only one kind of variable in JavaScript (created using var), there are a number of distinct objects that a variable can hold (Number, Date, String, Boolean, etc.). These objects are different from basic primitives in that the objects have additional properties and methods. Listing 4.5 illustrates the creation of several different object types.

```
<SCRIPT>
<!--
1: var x;
2: x=new Number(3);
3: x=new Array(5);
4: x=new Date("12/25/2001");
5: x=new String("some string");
6: x=new Boolean(false);
7:
8: x=new Object(); /* all types above inherits
9:                     from the Object type */
//-->
</SCRIPT>
```

Listing 4.5   Using the new keyword in JavaScript

Don't be confused by the presence of new; this keyword will be explained in the next section. Also, the line numbers on the left margin are included so particular lines can be referenced in the next topic; the line numbers are not part of the JavaScript.

All data types in JavaScript can optionally be created using the keyword new. Using new is, however, not necessary (or preferable) in most circumstances, especially in situations where you simply want to create a primitive such as a string, number, or boolean variable and assign it values as demonstrated in Listing 4.4. Keep in mind that all data types in JavaScript are really objects and, as such, can be declared using new in the fashion of Listing 4.5. The new keyword assigns a fresh memory space for the object.

You will note that in lines 2 though 5 of Listing 4.5 we are passing in an argument to a particular object instance as we create it. In line 2, for example, we are creating a new number that will have the value "3." In line 3, we are creating an array that will contain five elements, and in line 4 we are creating a new Date object that will have the initial value of 12/25/2001. Developers familiar with object-oriented languages such as C++ or Java should understand that we are creating a new object and initializing it by passing values into its constructor. The constructor is a method called whenever a new instance of the object is created. The method usually performs some sort of initialization operation. For example, the constructor for the Date object (line 4) sets the value equal to 12/25/2001.

Object Features

Because we know that all variables in JavaScript are objects, we can take advantage of certain features that objects offer beyond those of ordinary primitive types. For one thing, objects can have methods. Examine the following:

```
<SCRIPT>
  <!--
    var x;
    x=3;

    alert( x.toString() );
  //-->
</SCRIPT>
```

Listing 4.6   Calling an object's method

Even though x is holding a simple numerical value, 3, we can call the toString()function as a method of x and convert the number into a text string for display. The toString() method is one of a series of methods that all JavaScript objects support. We will encounter many more of these methods in this CodeNote, and a complete list can be found on the CodeNotes website at ⟡UI040002.

Building an Object at Runtime
A more subtle feature of JavaScript objects is that they can be built on the fly. Examine the following:

```
<SCRIPT>
  <!--
    var address;
    address=new Object;
    address.Street="Somani Way";
    address.Phone="213-254-3652";
  //-->
</SCRIPT>
```

Listing 4.7   Accessing an object's properties

The code shown in Listing 4.7 might seem odd to practitioners of other languages. We seem to be defining a class in the process of actually using it. In effect, we are building a class on the fly. While this may seem unusual to developers who are used to working with compiled languages, it is not all that strange for developers familiar with interpreted languages such as SmallTalk. In JavaScript, the simple act of referencing a property and assigning a value to it has the effect of actually creating the property on the object. Remember, variables in JavaScript never need to be formally declared before they can be used. This same rule applies to properties of objects.

One important thing to note about Listing 4.7 is that we have not created a proper class called address. All we have really done is created a new Object, called it address, and appended properties to that particular instance of the object and no other. As it is written, we could not, elsewhere in script, expect another address object to have Street and Phone properties. This takes us into the realm of Object-Oriented JavaScript, which is beyond the scope of this chapter, but if you are interested in reading further, see CodeNotes pointer ⟡UI040003.

Before we move on, you may have noticed that we are creating a new instance of an Object and assigning it to the address variable (address=newObject). The address variable must reference a JavaScript Object; otherwise, it will not be allowed to have properties and your browser will return an error saying something like "address is not an object." This is one instance where the use of the new keyword is absolutely required.

Functions

Functions are the cornerstone of almost every development language. Fortunately, functions in JavaScript have syntax that is similar to functions in most popular languages:

```
<SCRIPT>
<!--
  function add(x,y)
  {
    return x+y;
  }
  alert( add(3,4) );
//-->
</SCRIPT>
```

Listing 4.8   Defining and calling a function

First of all, the function keyword is all that is necessary to indicate that a function is being declared. Second, remembering that JavaScript is loosely typed, it makes sense that the function in Listing 4.8 does not provide data types for its arguments, x and y. On the same note, the function can simply return what it likes without formally declaring the type of its return value. If you want to write a function that does not have a return type, simply omit the return line. These details aside, JavaScript functions appear to be rather ordinary looking and, indeed, they are quite simple to learn.

Passing Arguments by Reference and Value

JavaScript has adopted a paradigm very similar to Java's when it comes to passing arguments into a function. Passing an argument by value means that a copy is made of whatever variable you pass into a function, and it is this copy that is passed in and modified by the function, leaving the original unchanged. Passing by reference, on the other hand, means that the variable you pass into a function can actually be permanently changed by the function.

Some languages, such as C and C++, allow you (via pointer notation) to specify which method (by value or by reference) you prefer for each argument being passed into a function. JavaScript, on the other hand, makes this choice for you, and the rule is simple: only proper objects, arrays, and functions are passed by reference. Everything else (numbers, dates, strings, booleans, etc.) is passed by value. As it is with Java, if you absolutely need to pass a primitive type by reference, you can use an array of that type with one element, as illustrated in Listing 4.9:

```
<HTML>
<SCRIPT>
<!--
  function byRef(z) {
    //arrays are zero-based
    z[0]=z[0]+1;
  }
  //Try it out by passing an array
  x=new Array(1);
  x[0]=3;  //JavaScript arrays are 0-based
  alert("Old value is " + x[0]);
  byRef(x);
  alert("New value is " + x[0]);
//-->
</SCRIPT>
</HTML>
```

Listing 4.9   Passing parameters by value and by reference

You should notice that the byRef() function does not have a return type. Therefore, only values that are passed by reference should be affected by the function. As demonstrated by the changing value of x[0], arrays are passed by reference. You can certainly force a primitive to be passed by reference using this sort of notation. Generally, however, it is best to design your functions with JavaScript value/reference rules in mind and avoid the single value array notation.

Functions as Objects
In JavaScript, functions, like every other data type, are objects. In other words, functions may be held in variables and even passed in as arguments to other functions. For example, examine Listing 4.10:

```
<script>
<!--
  x=3;
  f=new Function("x","return ++x");
  alert( f(x) );
//-->
</script>
```

Listing 4.10   Passing a function as a parameter

In the fourth line of Listing 4.10 we are actually creating a new function on the fly and assigning it to a variable f. We have to use Function with a capital F, because we are actually creating a new Function object. When you declare a function normally, you use the lowercase function keyword. Because functions are objects, and f, like any JavaScript variable, may hold any object including a newly created Function, f can be executed just as if we declared it formally, as we did in Listing 4.8.

The observant reader might also conclude from the fourth line of Listing 4.10 that it is possible to construct functions dynamically while a JavaScript program is running. This is correct: the second argument of the Function object's constructor is a string holding the actual code of the function, and strings, of course, can easily be built as a program runs. The actual prototype for the Function constructor lists all the function's arguments before the actual function definition:

```
var f2 = new Function(arg1, arg2, ... argN, functionbody);
```

The last parameter is always the body of the function.

Creating a function dynamically is useful, but a function can still be assigned to a variable and used even if it has been formally declared, as illustrated in Listing 4.11:

```
function addone(x)
{
  return ++x;
}

f=addone;
alert( f(x) );
```

Listing 4.11   Assigning a formally declared function to a variable

Now that we have established that a function is an object, it follows that a function, like any object, may be passed in as a parameter to another function. This is shown in Listing 4.12.

```
<script>
<!--
function somefunc()
{
  alert("Hi There!");
}
```

```
function execute(x)
{
  if( typeof(x) == "function")
  {
    x.call();
  }
  else
  {
    alert( "Argument not a function.");
  }
}

execute(test); //will print "Hi There" in a message box
//-->
</script>
```

Listing 4.12   Passing a function as a parameter to another function

In Listing 4.12 you can see the rationale for the call() method; it is used to execute a function passed in as an argument. You will also note the use of JavaScript's typeof() method, which returns a string indicating the data type that a given variable is currently referencing. When a function is passed into execute() as the parameter x, the typeof() function returns the literal string "function." If x contained a simple number, say 3, typeof() would have returned "number" and we would have fallen through to the else statement, resulting in message box saying "Argument not a function."

Other points to note: As with C++, the double equal (==) is used to determine equality, and the single equal sign (=) is used solely for assignment. JavaScript's if..else structure is also demonstrated here; it is identical to the if..else constructs of Java, C, C++, and other languages. Finally, be careful with capitalization. The typeof() method does not return the object type (Function, Number, etc.); rather, it returns the underlying arbitrary string that is always lowercase (function, number, etc.).

The this Object

Before we move on from discussing functions, it is important to talk about this. Java and C++ developers should already be familiar with the this keyword. In both languages, this can be thought of as a variable that always holds a reference pointing to the particular class instance using the this keyword. If, for example, a Java class wished to pass a

reference to itself to another class, it could simply pass the other class its
this variable.

In JavaScript, this has much the same role; but there is a twist. Examine Listing 4.13:

```
<script>
<!--
  function setinfo(name, phone)
  {
    this.name=name;
    this.phone=phone;
  }
//-->
</script>
```

Listing 4.13   Declaring a function that will use the this *keyword*

A JavaScript function like that shown in Listing 4.13 might look confusing to a C++ or Java programmer. After all, in these languages the
this pointer makes sense only in the context of a member function in an
object. Java doesn't allow stand-alone functions in the first place, and
while C++ does allow stand-alone functions, the this keyword may be
used only in a member function of an object.

If you remember that JavaScript is interpreted and not compiled, you
can think of a JavaScript this as a "future-this." In other words, the
setinfo() function is not part of an object, so this has no meaning, but
the setinfo() function may be associated with an object in the future.
When (or if) that happens, this will have meaning, as illustrated in
Listing 4.14:

```
<HTML>
<script>
<!--
  function setInfo(name, phone)
  {
    this.name=name;
    this.phone=phone;
  }
//Line numbers added for reference only.
//Remove the numbers to run code
1: address=new Object;
2: address.setAddressInfo=setInfo;
3:
4: address.setAddressInfo("bob","212-234-2342");
```

```
5:
6: alert(address.name +" , "+ address.phone);
//-->
</script>
</HTML>
```

Listing 4.14   Using a function that uses the this *keyword*

In this example, the setAddressInfo() function assigns values to variables that should be part of an Object (this.name and this.phone). However, until line 2, the setInfo() function is not assigned to any particular Object. By assigning setInfo to the setAddressInfo property on the address object, we link the setInfo() method to the object. Not only does this assignment provide a context for the this keyword in setInfo, it will also automatically create name and phone properties on the address object, if they weren't already there. Line 4 calls the setAddressInfo() property, which automatically passes the arguments to setInfo(), which sets the name and phone properties on the address object. Thus, line 6 will produce a message box reading "bob, 212-234-2432," even though we never explicitly added name or phone properties to the address object.

Looping and Control Structures

Like almost all popular languages, JavaScript has structures for looping (for..next, do..while) and control (if..else, switch..case). The syntax of these structures in JavaScript is almost identical to those of C++ and Java, so some simple code examples should suffice to give you the hang of working with these constructs. Listing 4.15 illustrates a multipart if statement, or switch..case structure:

```
switch(x)
{
  case 1,4:
  alert("x is 1 or 4");
  break;

  case "Tuesday":
  alert("x is a string");
  break;

  default:
  alert("default");
}
```

Listing 4.15   switch..case in JavaScript

Note that, in JavaScript, multiple choices are allowed for each case line and a single switch construct can handle multiple data types for x (in this case, x can be a number or a string.)

As with C++ and Java, the break statement is usually necessary after each case statement. If a break is missing, then the code of all subsequent case statements will execute. For example, if x had a value of 4 but the break statement was missing after case 1,4, you would see a message box reading "x is a string" in addition to the "x is 1 or 4" message box." Both case 1,4 and case "Tuesday" would be executed.

A switch..case is helpful for complex decisions, as is the traditional if..else statement, shown here:

```
if (x=="Monday")
{
  alert("it is Monday");
}
else if (x=="Tuesday" || x=="Wednesday")
{
  alert("it is Tuesday or Wednesday");
}
else alert("some other day");
```

Listing 4.16   if..else in JavaScript

The if..else construct in Listing 4.16 will be familiar to developers of C, C++, Java, and other languages. Note that the || operator represents a logical OR. The symbol for a logical AND is &&.

Looping Structures

JavaScript has four constructs for looping: for..next, while, do..while, and for..in. We will demonstrate each in turn.

The for..next Structure

Using for..next, Listing 4.17 will display a 10 by 10 multiplication table:

```
var s;

for(i=1; i<=10; i++)
{
  for(j=1; j<=10; j++)
  {
    s=s+i*j + "\t" //tab char
  }
```

```
  s=s+"\n";
}
alert(s);
```

Listing 4.17   for loops in JavaScript

The basic for statement contains three parts: variable initialization, a check condition, and an action. In this example, the first for loop declares variable i and sets it equal to 1, ensures that i is less than or equal to 10, and increments i during each loop. The second loop performs the same tasks for the variable j.

The while and do..while Structures

Both while and do..while are looping constructs. The difference between the two is that the code block encapsulated in a do..while will always execute at least once, whereas the code in a while block may not execute at all. Both constructs are illustrated in Listing 4.18:

```
var i;
//example of do..while
do
{
  alert("i is: " + i);
  i++;
} while(i<10);

//example of while
while(i<10);
{
  alert("i is: " + i);
  i++;
}
```

Listing 4.18   A do .. while loop and a while loop

Unlike a for loop, a while or do..while block does not have a variable initialization or action section, and you must increment any values yourself.

The for..in Structure

The final JavaScript looping construct is for..in. The for..in construct is used to iterate through an object's properties. Specifically, the for (property in object) construct will return (as variable property) the name of every property attached to object. The syntax is a little strange, as the code in Listing 4.19 demonstrates.

```
//create an object on the fly
a=new Object();
a.name="Mike";
a.hobby="racing";
for(x in a) {
  alert( x = a[x] );
}
```

Listing 4.19   Looping with the for.. in construct

This fragment creates an alert box for each property, returning the property name and value. Properties on JavaScript objects are exposed through an array-like notation, where the index value is the property name and the array value is the property value. In fact, you can use the array notation on any object, even outside of a `for..in` block. However, the notation can be confusing, as it looks like you are working with a normal array. The next topic explores the peculiar nature of arrays in more detail.

Arrays

Arrays in JavaScript are objects and may have properties just like any other object. Because of the array-like notation for user-defined object properties, you can create the illusion of an array with a string-based index. The code in Listing 4.20 looks like it has three elements using a string-based index.

```
fruit = new Array(3);
fruit["apples"] = 3;
fruit["pears"] = 4;
fruit["bananas"] = 0;
```

Listing 4.20   An array with three properties

However, the `fruit` array actually has three user-defined properties and three empty elements. If we tried to access the first element (`fruit[0]`), the value would be undefined. In fact, Listing 4.20 is actually equivalent to:

```
fruit = new Array(3);
fruit.apples = 3;
fruit.pears = 4;
fruit.bananas = 0;
```

Listing 4.21   The fruit array revisited

If we wanted to add a value to the array in a valid, indexed position, we would have to use the [] notation with an integer value as the index.

Array size

The size of a JavaScript array can be set in several ways. First, you can use the array constructor to assign a starting size. However, JavaScript will dynamically resize an array based on the highest index value.

```
a=new Array(3);
alert("Starting Length" + a.length);
a[5]="Element with index 5";
alert("Ending Length" + a.length);
```

Listing 4.22   Array lengths

In the first alert message, the array length will be 3. However, in the second alert message, the array length will be 6. The a[5] assignment automatically resizes the array to six elements. As you may have guessed by now, JavaScript arrays are always zero-based.

JavaScript arrays are also sparse. That is, an array can be any size, regardless of the number of elements that are actually assigned. An array may be defined to have 99 elements, but it may have only three real values. This is one of the largest drawbacks to dynamically sized arrays.

Arrays and for..in

The for..in looping structure behaves in a somewhat strange fashion when used with arrays. In particular, the for..in structure will return all of the array's properties and any array elements that have been set. The array in Listing 4.23, for example has a length of 5, although only the first two elements have been set. Using for..in will return elements a[0] and a[1]:

```
//create a new array of 5 elements
a=new Array(5);
a[0]=12;
a[1]=27;

for(x in a) alert( x + " = " + a[x]);
```

Listing 4.23   Using different object types as array indexes

In other words, the for..in structure can be very convenient for iterating through valid array elements, provided that the array does not have any assigned properties.

EXAMPLE

In this example, we will demonstrate how the concepts we have described so far can be combined to create a simple web page showing the values of squaring each of 0, 2, 4, 6, and 8. The boldfaced line uses the Document Object Model (discussed in the topic "The Document Object Model" in Chapter 5) to add new text to the HTML document (using the document.write() function). The first step in this process was to create an array of size 10. Then, in each even array index, we inserted the value of the index squared (i.e, we set a[2] to 2 times 2). Finally, we looped through all elements in the array (using the for..in construct) to display only the initialized values.

```
<html>
<body>
<SCRIPT language="JavaScript">
var a = new Array(10);
for (i=0;i<a.length; i+=2) {
  a[i] = i*i;
} // for
for (x in a) {
  document.write(x + " squared equals " + a[x] + "<br>");
} // for
//-->
</SCRIPT>
</body>
</html>
```

Listing 4.24   Script to generate even squares

The output from Listing 4.24 is shown in Figure 4.1.

HOW AND WHY

Can I Have Multiple Sections of JavaScript within the Same HTML File?
Yes, you can have as many sections of JavaScript as you require. Just make sure that all of your code appears between <SCRIPT> and </SCRIPT> tags. This is shown in Listing 4.25.

This listing displays alert messages counting up from 1 to 5, displays HTML text, and then counts down from 5 to 1.

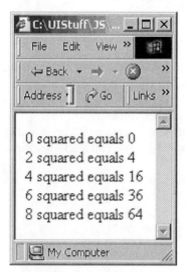

Figure 4.1   Output of Listing 4.24

```
<HTML>
<SCRIPT>
<!--
  for (i=1;i<=5;i++) {
    alert(i);
  }
//-->
</SCRIPT>

Count Up complete
<SCRIPT>
<!--
  for (i=5; i>0; i--) {
    alert(i);
  }
//-->
</SCRIPT>
</HTML>
```

Listing 4.25   Multiple Script tags

Does My Function Code Have to Appear in My Code before I Call It?
You can call a JavaScript function if:

- It is defined in the same <SCRIPT> block as your code. Your function may be declared before or after the call to the function.

• It is defined in a <SCRIPT> block that is prior to your current <SCRIPT> block.

If you try to call a function that is defined in a <SCRIPT> block after the current <SCRIPT> block, you will generate an error.

Does JavaScript Handle Exceptions?

The syntax for JavaScript exceptions is very similar to the syntax for exception handling in Java, as you can see in Listing 4.26.

```
// throws an exception if b == 0
function divideBy (a,b) {
  if (b==0)
    throw "Can't divide by 0"
  else
    alert(a/b);
} // function

/* assign values to a and b here, exception will be thrown
   when we call divideBy because b = 0 */
a = 5
b = 0
// attempt to call divideBy
try {
  divideBy(a,b);
} catch(exception) {
  alert("The function didn't work properly: " + exception);
} finally {
  alert("The math section is done");
} // try
```

Listing 4.26   Exception handling in Java

Notice in the divideBy() function, an exception is thrown by simply using the throw keyword. The string after throw ("Can't divide by 0") is a message used to describe the exception. If you are familiar with programming exceptions, the try ... catch ... finally works as expected. The code within the try block is executed unless an exception is thrown. If an exception is thrown, the catch section of the code is executed. The finally section is always executed regardless of whether an error was thrown.

Unlike some programming languages, such as Java, there is only a single exception type. However, if you wish to handle multiple exception types, you can use if statements within the catch block as shown in

Listing 4.27. The first `catch` statement will only be executed if the value of the exception is "Can't divide by 0." If the exception has any other value, the second `catch` block will be executed. Catch blocks without a conditional statement will always be executed and will prevent other `catch` blocks from executing. As a result, if you have a `catch` statement without a conditional block, it should always be placed after conditional block statements.

```
// same code as the start of Listing 4.27
try {
   divideBy(a,b);
} catch(exception if (exception == "Can't divide by 0") {
   alert("divideBy error");
} catch(exception) {
   alert("Not a divide by error");
} // catch
```

Listing 4.27   Using conditional catch blocks

Exceptions are a new feature to JavaScript and, as a result, they are only supported by Netscape 6.X and IE 5.0+.

DESIGN NOTES

Extensive Testing

All browsers provide different support for JavaScript. Browsers even differ in how they handle unsupported features. Because of these two facts, it is very important that you test your web pages on all browsers your clients may be using.

Script Libraries

If you're designing a web application and find that many of your pages are using the same client-side functionality, you should consider using JavaScript libraries. Rather than duplicating the same code for each HTML file, you can reference a single external script file containing nothing but JavaScript code (i.e., a simple text file, without any `<script>` tags). Script libraries are specified with a `.js` two-character extension.

To load an external library file, simply add an `src` attribute to your `<script>` tag in your HTML document:

```
<script language="JavaScript" src="myFunctions.js"></script>
```

Listing 4.28   Referencing an external script library

This will cause the file myFunctions.js to be loaded with your HTML page, and any script within the file can be referenced or executed as if it were part of your page.

You should avoid putting script statements between the script tags that reference an src library file. The src attribute is effectively translated to "open this file, and place the entire contents inline with the current web page." If you add your own code inside the same script block, your page will be much less readable (and maintainable) than if you simply create a separate script block for your JavaScript that is local to the page, as illustrated in Listing 4.29.

```
<script language="JavaScript" src="myFunctions.js"></script>
<script language="JavaScript"
  function doSomething() { //do something }
</script>
```

Listing 4.29   Combining script libraries with local JavaScript

External library capabilities are available on IE 3.02+ and Netscape 3+.

SUMMARY

The basics of JavaScript are relatively straightforward, especially if you are familiar with other programming languages such as C, C++, or Java. JavaScript, like Perl, uses loosely typed variables to represent data; any variable can be a number, a string, an array, a function, or any other data type, depending on the value you assign it.

JavaScript's control and looping structures are virtually identical to those in many other languages, with the addition of the for..in structure that allows you to iterate through members of an object.

Functions in JavaScript (which are also objects) can be declared using the Function keyword, and can receive and return any kind of variable without having to be predefined. Functions, objects, and arrays are always passed by reference into functions; all other data types are passed by value.

This topic should have familiarized you with the basic syntax of JavaScript. JavaScript is used throughout web pages for tasks ranging from validating data (using regular expressions) to creating dynamic effects (DHTML). These advanced uses of JavaScript are illustrated in the next topic and in Chapter 5.

Topic: Regular Expressions

The JavaScript RegExp object is a very powerful tool for performing pattern matching on text. You can use the RegExp object to search through text, replace parts of text, reformat data, and validate user-entered information.

Now that you have basic JavaScript under your belt, this section will show you how to add functionality to your web pages by leveraging the pattern-matching abilities of regular expressions.

CONCEPTS

What Is a Regular Expression?

Anyone who has ever typed dir *.exe at a DOS prompt or ls * on a Unix command line has used a form of pattern matching. In the aforementioned cases, you are performing pattern matching via the operating system's set of regular expressions, where the * is a special character meaning "anything at all" and therefore dir *.exe will return a list of all files ending in .exe. The * symbol and many others can be put together to form a *regular expression* that can be used by JavaScript to search, parse, find, and replace blocks of characters in an HTML document. Let's take a look at some examples.

Listing 4.30 demonstrates how you can make good use of regular expressions if you and your best friend, Sheldon, have a falling out and you want your other friend, Alim, to replace Sheldon as your new favorite.

```
<script>

//note that '+' is a string concatenation operator in JavaScript
s="Sheldon is my best friend.  Shelly and me go way back. " +
  "Shelster is my pal";

//Means "all words beginning with Shel and ending with any
//number of letters up until the next blank space is found
r=RegExp("Shel\\w*\\b","ig");

//all strings have a replace method.
s2=s.replace(r, "Alim");
```

```
alert(s2);
</script>
```

Listing 4.30   Using regular expressions to replace occurrences of strings

There are a few new items of note in Listing 4.30. For one thing, you will notice the use of the RegExp object. The RegExp object contains a regular expression and can be passed into functions that can use regular expressions to search through HTML. In this listing, the RegExp object is passed into the string.replace() method.

The constructor of a RegExp object takes two arguments. The first is the regular expression as a string. In our case, this string is "Shel\\w*\\b," the details of which will be explained shortly. The second argument will always be "i," "g," or "ig." This argument is a flag indicating whether a search should be case-insensitive (i) and/or global (g). A global search continues processing after encountering the first matching instance. If you omit the second argument, the RegExp will default to case-sensitive and local (stop at first match).

Therefore, the RegExp object in Listing 4.30 has been defined to match all words beginning with "Shel," regardless of case, throughout the entire string. When the RegExp object is passed into the replace() method of the string s2, the strings "Sheldon," "Shelly," and "Shelster" will all be replaced with "Alim." As previously stated, "Shel\\w*\\b" requires further explanation. In order for you to understand what this expression means, you need a crash course in JavaScript regular expression notation.

Regular Expression Notation
Regular expressions in JavaScript follow a notation that is similar to Perl's. This notation is explained in the following concepts.

Square Brackets []
Square brackets can contain any number of different characters that constitute an allowable match. For example:

```
s="Canadians spell it 'apologise', but the American spelling
is 'apologize.' with a 'z'.";

r = new RegExp("apologi[sz]e", "ig");

x = s.match(r); //finds and separates matches

for each (index in x) {
```

```
alert( x[index] );
}
```

Listing 4.31   Matching multiple occurrences of a pattern using regular expressions

The code in Listing 4.31 uses a regular expression that will match both spellings of the word "apologize." Note the use of the brackets [sz], which indicate that the expression should match on either "s" or "z" in this position of the word. Listing 4.31 also demonstrates the use of the String object's match() method. The match() method finds matches to a regular expression and returns an array of matched strings.

Here is another small example demonstrating how you can specify a range of characters with a hyphen:

```
s="I am taking Vitamin C for colds, Vitamin B for strength, "
+
"and also Vitamin E.";

var r=new RegExp("\\bVitamin\\s[A-E]\\b", "gi");

matches=s.match(r);

s2="I am presently taking the following Vitamins:" +
    matches.join(" , ");

alert(s2);
```

Listing 4.32   Specifying a range of characters

You will notice that the regular expression in Listing 4.32 uses the bracket notation to indicate that any capital letter, A through E inclusive, constitutes an acceptable match. The same method can be used with numbers (i.e., [0-9]). You will also note the \b and \s characters in the expression. The \b indicates a word boundary. The text following the \b must be its own word; it can't be text at the end of some other string. In other words, \b is roughly equivalent to "this text must be the first character in the string, or there must be a space here." The \s means a whitespace character. As we will see soon, you can think of \s as just a shortcut for a bracketed group of possible whitespace characters. In this expression we are saying that we expect that the word "Vitamin" and the vitamin type (A-E) will have a space or some form of whitespace character between them. We will look at \ codes in a little more detail in the next section.

One final feature to note in Listing 4.32 is the use of the array object's join() method. join() is a convenience function that will concatenate the elements of an array into a single string where each element will be separated by the character(s) you pass as an argument to the join() method. The resulting string of this listing will therefore be, "I am presently taking the following Vitamins: Vitamin C, Vitamin B, Vitamin E." If you wanted to build your own string from the elements of the array, you could use a for..next construct as shown here:

```
//An alternative to join(): for..next
//cont. from Listing 4.32

s2="I am presently taking the following Vitamins:"
for(i=0; i<matches.length - 1; i++)
{
  s2=s2+" , "+ matches[i];
}
alert(s2);
```

Listing 4.33   An alternative to using the join() method

As you can see, the join() method saves several lines of code for simple string concatenation.

"\" Characters

The \ character is always followed by exactly one character and can mean one of three things in a regular expression. The first use of the \ is to represent a *literal* character; that is, a character that is either not printable (line feeds, carriage returns, tab, etc.) or a character that is also used in the syntax of a formal regular expression ("(," "*," "[," etc.). A complete list of literals can be found at ⊶UI040007.

The second use of \ is to represent a *character* class. You may recall from Listing 4.32 that we used a \s character class to denote that there would be some kind of whitespace between the word "Vitamin" and the vitamin type. The \s code, however, is just a short way of saying [\t\n\f\r\v]; these two elements are equivalent, but \s is more concise and makes for regular expressions that are easier to read. Technically, anything inside square brackets constitutes a custom character class.

Table 4.1 is a partial list of character class shortcuts (see ⊶UI040004 for a complete list). You should know that for every lowercase character class shown in this table, there is a corresponding uppercase version that

Character Class Shortcut	Class of Characters
\w	[a-zA-Z0-9_] (any alphanumeric including underscore)
\s	[\t\n\f\r\v] (any whitespace characters)
\d	[0=9] (any digit)

Table 4.1   A list of commonly used character class shortcuts

means exactly the opposite. So, where \s means any character that is a whitespace character, \S means any character that is not a whitespace character. The same is true of \W (not an alphanumeric) and \D (not a digit).

The third and final use of \ is to denote certain *anchor* characters, specifically \b (and its negation, \B), which means match up until the end of the word. Recall in Listing 4.32 that we placed a \b on either side of the regular expression \bVitamin\s[A-E]\b, indicating that we wanted a match on "Vitamin" *only* if it was a word on its own. Thus, "multivitamin A" would not be matched by this expression unless you removed the \b at the start of the expression. Similarly, "Vitamin B1" would not be matched by this expression since the \b at the end indicates that the pattern will match only if the word ends after the A-E character. Technically, \b matches on any nonword (\W) character. In other words, any character that is not a number or a letter technically satisfies the word-boundary anchor condition. Other anchor characters include \^ (start of the string) and \$ (end of the string). A regular expression for "Vitamin" on a single line would be "\^Vitamin\$."

Curly Brackets {}
Curly brackets specify an explicit minimum and maximum number of allowed occurrences for a pattern. For example, the regular expression \d{3,4} matches any group of three or four digits, \d{3,} matches any group of three or more digits, and \d{3} matches any group of *exactly* three digits. We will revisit the concept of regular expression repetition in the next section as well as in the example at the end of this topic.

*Occurrence Counter Characters (?, +, and *)*
These special characters also have to do with repetition. The ? character matches if a pattern occurs zero or one time; + matches if a pattern occurs one or more times; and * matches if a pattern occurs zero or more times. We'll put these symbols to use in the following example, and it will become perfectly clear.

Example

Now that you understand basic JavaScript and regular expressions, let's take the different elements of the language and put them together to demonstrate how JavaScript can actually be used in a web application.

When entering data in a web-based form, it is common for users to make mistakes. After clicking the Submit button, the server will normally examine the values in the fields using server-side scripts and will inform the client of any field values that are missing or badly formed.

Using JavaScript, however, it is possible to perform this validation on the client side and save our server the processing time required to perform form validation. Suppose we have a web form that asks the user for his or her phone number, but we want to make certain that the user enters a number with a form valid for U.S. or European phone numbers. Examine the following code:

```
<html>
<body>
<script>
  function ValidatePhone(p)
  {
    //Note that you can specify regular expressions between
    //single slashes / <your reg expression here> / instead of
    //between quotes if you choose.
    r=RegExp(/^((\(?\d{3}\))|(\d{3}))?\s?\d{3}[\-.]?\d{4}$/);
    if( r.test(p) == false)
    {
      alert("Phone must be in the form (nnn)nnn-nnnn or "+
        "valid European format.");
      //return focus to text box
      document.Form1.PhoneNum.focus();
    }
  }
</script>
<form Name="Form1" method="POST" action="submit_page.asp">
  <p>
    <input type="text" name="PhoneNum" size="20"
      onBlur="ValidatePhone(document.Form1.PhoneNum.value)"
      value="test">
  </p>
  <p>
    <input type="submit" value="Submit" name="B1">
```

```
      <input type="reset" value="Reset" name="B2">
   </p>
</form>
</body>
</html>
```

Listing 4.34 validate.html

Most of the language elements of Listing 4.34 should be familiar to you by now. Some elements that are new are bold in the code. In essence, we have created a basic form with a single text field that takes in a phone number. When the text box loses focus (that is, when the user attempts to go to another field or button in the HTML page), the text field's DHTML onBlur event will be triggered (in bold). We will cover DHTML events and properties in depth in Chapter 5, but for now, note that we respond to this event by calling our ValidatePhone method (passing in the fully qualified name of our text field as an argument). The ValidatePhone method tests the value against a regular expression for a correctly formed phone number using the RegExp.test() method. If the data does not conform to a proper phone number, we do not allow focus to change (document.Form1.T1.focus()), thereby forcing the user to enter a properly configured phone number.

HOW AND WHY

When I Use "." in My Regular Expressions, Why Does It Match More Characters Than "."?
The "." is a special character in regular expressions. It matches any single character except the new line (\n) character (e.g., symbols, numbers, letters). This matching is often used when validating user names. For example, the regular expression in Listing 4.35 matches all strings consisting of four or more characters.

```
r = RegExp(/....+/);
```

Listing 4.35 A regular expression for matching four or more characters of any type

In order to match a "." instead of all characters, you have to use "\." as with other special characters.

When Should I Enclose a RegExp in Quotes, and When Can I Use Forward Slashes?
You may have noticed that several examples used the forward slash character to indicate a regular expression. This character is actually a

shortcut used by JavaScript. You can actually define a regular expression three ways:

```
//Using the string-based constructor. Must use \\
r = new RegExp("\\bVitamin\\s[A-E]\\b")
//use the / notation:
r = new RegExp(/\bVitamin\s[A-E]\b/);
//use the implicit translation
r = /\bVitamin\s[A-E]\b/;
```

Listing 4.36   RegExp constructors

All three statements generate a RegExp object containing the same pattern. As you might guess, the forward slash notation can be very handy if your expression contains many escape characters.

DESIGN NOTES

Other Common Regular Expressions

It should be apparent by now that regular expressions are powerful tools for client-side validation. We've shown one example for validating phone numbers. There are many other common types of strings that can be validated using regular expressions. Some possibilities are shown in Table 4.2.

	Regular Expression	**Valid String**
E-mail	/^.+\@.+\..+$/	a@b.c
Date	/^\d{1,2}(\-|\/|\.)\d{1,2}\1\d{4}$/	mm/dd/yyyy
ZIP code	/(^\d{5}$)\|(^\d{5}-\d{4}$)/	99999 or 99999-9999
Time	/^([1-9]|1[0-2]):[0-5]\d(:[0-5]\d(\.\d{1,3})?)?$/	HH:MM or HH:MM:SS or HH:MM:SS.mmm

Table 4.2   Common regular expressions

For an extended list of regular expressions, consult the CodeNotes website at ♻UI040005.

Alerting the User

When performing client-side form validation, it is important to inform users when they have entered an invalid field. An obvious choice would be an alert box.

```
window.alert("Invalid expression");
```

Listing 4.37   Using an alert box

However, this may prove irritating for a user when he or she has filled in several fields incorrectly. Having multiple alert boxes pop up is annoying. Alternatively, there is only so much you can place in one alert box.

A more savvy error-handling technique could be to output a dynamic list of invalid fields or highlight those field boxes that have not been filled in correctly using DHTML. Chapter 5 will give you the tools you need to accomplish this.

For an example of form-field validation using DHTML, see the CodeNotes website at ⌒CN⟩UI000406.

SUMMARY

Regular expressions are used for pattern matching in JavaScript. Regular expressions are created by passing two parameters into the constructor of a RegExp object: a string representing the expression, and options indicating whether or not you want to search case-insensitively ("i") and/or multiple instances ("g"). Special characters in regular expressions are prefixed by a slash ("/") and represent different groups of characters, such as alphanumeric characters (\w), digits (\d), or whitespace characters. These special characters can also represent character classes, which are groups of special characters sharing a common theme. Regular expressions are useful in web pages, particularly when you are designing forms, as they can be used to validate form fields on the client side, as opposed to using server-side scripts.

Chapter Summary

JavaScript is a scripting language that can be used within the HTML code for your web pages to add functionality and dynamism. JavaScript code appears between <script> and </script> tags in your code and should generally be encompassed by HTML-style comments (<!-- -->) to avoid confusion for non-JavaScript-compatible browsers.

JavaScript takes many features from other popular programming languages. Its grammar for control and looping structures is very similar to those of C++ and Java. Its loosely typed variables are modeled after the Perl scripting language; all variables in JavaScript are declared using the var keyword and take on a particular data type only when a value is assigned to them.

Although technically all variables in JavaScript are objects, it is usually safe to consider types such as strings and numbers to be "primitive" types. Functions, arrays, and proper objects are all objects as well. Every object in JavaScript has a set collection of methods that can be executed on it. Every kind of variable can be passed into, and returned by, a function.

JavaScript also makes use of a special RegExp object that allows you to perform pattern matching on your HTML, allowing you to perform tasks such as form validation on the client side.

Please remember that this chapter is by no means a full JavaScript reference. It is simply intended to give you an introduction to how the language works and how you can leverage it to improve your web user interface. Chapter 5 will discuss Dynamic HTML (DHTML), which, in combination with JavaScript, can be used to further manipulate the contents of your web pages.

Chapter 5

—

DHTML AND THE DOCUMENT
OBJECT MODEL

The first thing to understand about Dynamic HyperText Markup Language (DHTML) is that it is *not* a language or a standard. Rather, DHTML is a term used by browser vendors to refer to any client-side extensions to HTML that allow web pages to be dynamic, that is, to change depending on the actions of the web page user. It is best to think of DHTML as a grouping of technologies that include scripting languages such as JavaScript and VBScript, stylesheet languages such as Cascading Style Sheets (CSS), and the Document Object Model (DOM).

The DOM is the real heart of DHTML. If you have ever programmed any form of event-driven user interface, the DOM should be very easy to understand. By event-driven, we are referring to the common paradigm whereby a graphical object such as a form will have a predefined series of events (and properties) such as onClick (when the form is clicked), onMouseOver (when the mouse cursor is moved over a portion of the form), and many others. These events act as bindings whereby you can "hook" your own code such that when the event occurs, your code is executed. For an HTML page in a browser, the browser's DOM provides the event hooks, and you can attach your JavaScript code to respond to these events. In addition to providing event hooks, the DOM also defines page and control properties that can be read and manipulated. For example, it is possible to change the caption on a button dynamically using the button's DOM property value. The DHTML DOM is now a World

Wide Web Consortium (W3C) standard, and is supported by the most recent versions of Netscape, Internet Explorer, and Opera.

CSS, on the other hand, is a language used to identify formatting that can be applied to HTML elements. By moving formatting out of your HTML and into a CSS, you can reuse common formats and even change formats globally for your entire website. Like the DOM, CSS is a W3C standard and is supported by most modern browsers.

The various components of DHTML are extremely important in designing high-quality web-based user interfaces. Unfortunately, the power of DHTML provides a tremendous potential for abuse. As you read this chapter, keep the design principles from Chapter 3 in mind. DHTML should be used to enhance your website in subtle ways. Gratuitous use of DHTML, however, can distract the user and make the web experience very difficult.

SIMPLE APPLICATION

The following code sample uses three event handlers to illustrate different events. Specifically, the page contains a simple URL hyperlink to www.codenotes.com. This link will become red when the mouse is moved over it, and blue when the mouse is no longer over it. If you click the URL, you will be presented with a message box reading, "Boing!"

```
<html>
  <head>
    <script>
      <!--
      function boing() { alert("BOING!");}
      function brighten(e) { e.srcElement.style.color="red" }
      function darken(e) { e.srcElement.style.color="blue" }
      //-->
    </script>
  </head>
  <body>
    <!-- The following anchor has event handlers in it -->
    <a href="http://www.codenotes.com"
        onClick="boing();"
        onMouseOver="brighten(event);"
        onMouseOut="darken(event);">Click Here</a>
```

```
  </body>
</html>
```

Listing 5.1   simpleDHTML.html

There are a few things going on in Listing 5.1. You will notice that we are responding to the `onMouseOver` and `onMouseOut` event handlers (we are going to ignore the `onClick` event handler for the moment). In both cases, we are providing JavaScript indicating that `brighten()` should be called when the `onMouseOver` fires, and `darken()` should be called when `onMouseOut` fires. In both cases, we are passing an `event` object as the argument. As we will see in subsequent sections, the `event` object has a property that holds a reference to the object associated with the event (the <a> tag in this case). For IE this property is the `srcElement` property, although for Netscape the property is named `currentTarget`. Passing the `event` object as an argument to the `brighten()` and `darken()` functions gives the functions the ability to dynamically change the stylistic property of the <a> tag, such that it can become red or blue.

Topic: Event Handlers

As shown in Listing 5.1, event handlers take the form of attributes, which can be added to HTML elements. Each type of HTML element has its own set of possible events. By trapping the appropriate event, you can create different functionality for conditions such as mouse clicks, lost focus, or changed values. This topic illustrates the use of the various types of event handlers.

CONCEPTS

Focus
Many of the event handlers deal in one way or another with the concept of focus. The control that has focus is the one that is currently active and intercepting user input. For example, a text box that has focus will turn any keystrokes into letters inside the text box, whereas a button that has focus might execute if the user presses the enter key. One, and only one, object can have the focus at any given time. In a simple web page with a text box and a button, for example, either the button, the text box, or the page itself will have focus.

An object can lose focus in several ways. The most common method is that the user clicks on another object, using the mouse. A control can also lose focus if the user presses the Tab key. The Tab key actually cycles through all of the objects that can have focus. Some controls, such as text boxes, may lose focus when the user presses the Enter key. You can also use the DOM to shift focus from one object to the next.

As mentioned previously, many events are tied to either gaining or losing focus. Keep this in mind as you read the remaining concepts in this topic.

Types of Handlers

Different HTML elements have different types of events. For example, a text field has an onChange event that executes when the text is modified, as shown in Listing 5.2.

```
<html>
<body>
<script>
  function Changed(e)
  {
    //Note: the 'value' property of a text field
    //holds the text the user typed in that field

    alert("The text changed! The new value is "+
      e.srcElement.value);
  }
</script>
<form Name="Form1" method="POST" action="submit_page.asp">
  <input type="text" name="T1" size="20"
    onChange="Changed(event)" value="test"></p>
</form>
</body>
</html>
```

Listing 5.2   Using the onChange event

The onChange event fires when the user makes a change to the text box and then clicks elsewhere, causing the text box to lose focus. In other words, this event fires only after the user performs two actions: changing the text and moving focus to a different object.

Note that while an onChange event makes sense for a text field (also FileUpload, Select, and TextArea elements), it does not make sense as an attribute for an element such as an anchor (<a>): the user can change a text field, but cannot change an <a> element. Here again, even though you may place any event handler you like as any attribute in any element, a handler that is paired with an inappropriate element will never fire. A complete list of elements and their permitted attributes can be found at °^{CN}UI050001. For the moment, however, here is a partial list of the most commonly used attributes:

- *Button clicks.* The onClick event handler will activate when the user left-clicks on the element. In early versions of browsers, it worked only for anchor (<a>) and button elements, but it now works for almost every element (including tables, images, and paragraphs). Related events include onDblClick, onMouseDown (when the user still has his or her finger pressed down on the mouse button after a click), and onMouseUp (when the user releases the button after onMouseDown).
- *Mouse motion.* The onMouseOver event activates when the mouse passes over the element of which onMouseOver is an attribute. Like onClick and its relatives, onMouseOver and its opposite, onMouseOut, are available on every visible element.
- *Focus.* The onBlur and onFocus events activate when objects on an HTML page lose and gain focus, respectively. As mentioned previously, loss of focus occurs when a particular element is active, and the user tabs to or clicks on another element. The onBlur method of the original element would be called, and then the onFocus method of the new element would be called.
- *Keyboard.* The onKeyDown, onKeyPress, and onKeyUp events activate when the user presses keys and/or releases keys. These handlers are extremely useful in text entry areas in forms because they can be used to control what characters a user is allowed to enter into a text box. For example, you could have onKeyPress check to see whether a character just typed is valid, and, if not, give an error message and disallow the key. The onKeyDown event activates when the key is pressed, and onKeyPress is activated immediately afterward. The onKeyUp event activates when you let go of the key. If you hold down a key until it begins autorepeating, onKeyDown and onKeyPress are activated repeatedly until you let go of the key.

Handler Properties

While it is very common to see event handlers as attributes of elements, there is another, perhaps more succinct, way of associating a handling function with an event handler. Handler properties are best demonstrated in code. Consider the simple event handler in Listing 5.3:

```
<script>
  function myFunc() { // function code }
</script>
<form>
  <input type="button" value="Click Here" onClick="myFunc();">
</form>
```

Listing 5.3   A simple way of handling the onClick event

Rather than link the event handler directly to the input element, you can use the DOM's handler properties to link the function programmatically:

```
document.forms[0].myButton.onclick = function myFunc() {
  // function code
}
</script>
<form>
  <input type="button" name="myButton" value="Click Here">
</form>
```

Listing 5.4   Handling the onClick method in a separate part of the HTML file

The first line of Listing 5.4 uses the DOM to link `myFunc()` to the `onClick` event for the button. The `document` keyword represents the complete HTML page, or the document. The `document` object is DOM's reference to the content of the current page, and many other objects reside "under" the `document` object. For example, a `document` may contain one or many forms (although conventionally we tend to have only one form per page). The `document.forms[0]` part references the first form in the document, and if we have only one form, `document.forms[0]` serves as a reference to that form. All the controls of an HTML page or DOM document will automatically be properties of the form in which they are declared. Thus `document.forms[0].myButton` is the unambiguous path to the `myButton` control. From here, we can read and manipulate the properties of the `myButton` control.

Note that if you take advantage of handler properties, your event-handling methods may be called directly from anywhere else in your code. You can always call handlers as object properties within your scripts, using the document object—for example: `document.forms[0]` `.buttonName.onMouseOver()`. You can also link many different controls to the same method. For example, you can create a standard `brighten()` and `darken()` method for `mouseOver` and `mouseOut` events and attach these functions to all of your controls ∘^{CN}↪UI050006.

The Event Object

Returning to Listing 5.1, you may recall that when an event handler fires, it is convenient to pass in an event object to your handling function. We saw that the event object has properties that contain useful information and hold valuable references (such as srcElement, which holds a reference to the element that has launched the event). But where does this useful object come from and what other useful properties does it have?

The event object is created each time an event handler is called, and is assigned properties depending on the circumstances of the event. For example, in the event of an onMouseOver, the event object contains a handle to the element from which it was called, the element from which the mouse moved before it was called, and other details including the name of the event itself. Thus, by using the properties of the event object intelligently, we can combine the brighten(), darken(), and boing() functions of Listing 5.1 such that we now have:

```html
<html>
  <head>
    <script>
      function DoTheRightThing(e)
      {
        if (e.type == "mouseover")
          e.srcElement.style.color="red"
        else if (e.type == "mouseout")
          e.srcElement.style.color="blue"
        else
          alert("Boing!");
      }
    </script>
  </head>
  <body>
    <!-- The following anchor has event handlers in it -->
    <a href="http://www.codenotes.com"
       onClick="DoTheRightThing(event);"
       onMouseOver="DoTheRightThing(event);"
       onMouseOut="DoTheRightThing(event);">Click Here</a>
  </body>
</html>
```

Listing 5.5   Using a single method to handle all events

In Listing 5.5 we can see how the event object's type property can allow a single function to handle multiple event types.

The event object has a number of properties. A complete list can be found at ⌕UI050002, and we will see many of the more important event properties used throughout this chapter.

Event Bubbling

In HTML, you frequently have elements that are nested in other elements. For example, a button exists in a form that itself may exist within a table. It may be that you want the onClick event to fire not just for the button, but for all three elements (button, form, and table) in succession; in other words, you want the event to bubble upward. In the following code, we have a button in a form in a table. When you click the button, the event will bubble up just as we have discussed:

```
<html>
<body>
<table onClick="alert('We've jumped up to the table')">
  <tr><td>
    <form onClick="alert('Now I am in the form')">
      <input type="button" value="Start Bubbling!"
        onClick=
          "alert('Bubbling beginning. I am in the button')">
    </form>
  </td></tr>
</table>
</body>
</html>
```

Listing 5.6   Nested events

If you try this code, you will see three message boxes bearing the text "Bubbling beginning. I am in the button," "Now I am in the form," and "Now I have jumped up to the table" messages.

Note that bubbling is the default behavior. Events in IE 5 and Netscape 6.0 will automatically bubble upward unless you specifically indicate that they should not. To stop bubbling, you need simply add the code event.cancelBubble=true; to your handling code. For example, in Listing 5.6, if we change this line:

```
<form onClick="alert('Now I am in the form!')">
```

Listing 5.7   Default bubbling

and add a little code such that we have:

```
<form onClick="alert('Now I am in the form!');
event.cancelBubble=true;">
```

Listing 5.8   No bubbling

then the onClick event will stop bubbling at the form level, and the table's onClick handler will never be called.

In Netscape 4.x events trickle down instead of bubbling up. Therefore, an event will pass through the window, document, and so on, first. The output in Listing 5.6 would therefore only display the "I am in the button" text in these versions. Netscape 6.0, however, exhibits bubbling-up behavior.

EXAMPLE

Suppose you want to implement an event handler that not only highlights text, but makes it larger when you pass the mouse over it. This is a common way of handling an onMouseOver. Not only does the color change, but the actual text style changes with it.

To accomplish this all you have to do is change a style property of the text. We'll attach a couple of event handlers to some paragraph tags to show this.

```
<html>
<head>

<script language="javascript">
  function genText(obj, increase)
  {
    if (increase)
    {
      obj.style.fontSize = '20px';
      obj.style.color = 'red';
    }
    else
    {
      obj.style.fontSize = '16px';
      obj.style.color = 'black',
    }
  }
</script>
```

```
</head>
<body>
  <p id='p1' style="font-size:16px"
     onMouseOver="genText(this, true)"
     onMouseOut="genText(this, false)">
     Here's some simple text</p>
  <p id='p2' style="font-size:16px"
     onMouseOver="genText(this, true)"
     onMouseOut="genText(this, false)">
     Here's some more text</p>
</body>
</html>
```

Listing 5.9   Implementing an onmouseover *to text*

The event handler genText() will increase or decrease the paragraph text and change the color, depending on whether an onMouseOver or onMouseOut event occurred.

Now suppose for some reason we want to be able to disable this event on the fly. We can use an onKeyPress event handler to handle our own custom disable key (let's use the letter "d").

```
//Insert into Listing 5.9 <script> block
function detectKey(e)
{
  if (window.navigator.appName == 'Netscape')
    src = e.which;
  else
    src = e.keyCode;
  if (src == '68')  // 'd' key in us ASCII
  {
    document.getElementById('p1').onMouseOver = null;
    document.getElementById('p1').onMouseOut = null;
  }
}
</script>
<!-- Replace <body> tag of Listing 5.9 with this -->
<body onKeyDown="detectKey(event)">
<!-- remainder of listing is the same as Listing 5.9 -->
</body>
</html>
```

Listing 5.10   Implementing an onkeydown *handler*

To implement this, the onKeyDown event must be handled at the <body> level, and then used to detect which key was pressed. Note the different implementation of the event object for both browsers. Netscape implements an event.which syntax to detect the ASCII value of the key pressed. IE uses an event.keyCode syntax for the same task. In this case, to disable the event handler for the first paragraph, we simply set the event handler equal to null.

HOW AND WHY

How Do I Add an Event Handler to Every Instance of a Particular Object Type?

The document.getElementsByTagName returns an array of elements that use a particular tag. For example, we can add an onClick event handler to every <p> tag using Listing 5.11:

```
function attachEvents()
{
  // Get all our <p> tags
  var tagCollection;
  tagCollection = document.getElementsByTagName('p');

  for (i=0; i<tagCollection.length; i++)
  {
    tagCollection[i].onClick = eventHandler;
  }
}

function eventHandler()
{
  // Service this event..
}
```

Listing 5.11   Getting all elements of a common type

The method returns a collection of all elements that are specified with the string "p". In this case, we are retrieving all nodes of type <p>. We can then iterate through the collection and attach our event handler function to each element, as shown in bold in Listing 5.11.

DESIGN NOTES

Subtle Effects and Smart Colors
When you use an onMouseOver event to highlight an object, use a subtle color transition. For example, following the rules from Chapter 3, a simple adjustment of the saturation or brightness from low to high makes an effective highlight. If you switch colors from, for example, blue to yellow, most users will find the effect disconcerting. Try the following code and see for yourself:

```
<html>
<head>
  <script>
    function good(e)
    {
      if (e.type == "mouseover")
        e.srcElement.style.color="#0000FF"
      else if (e.type == "mouseout")
        e.srcElement.style.color="#333399;"
    }
    function bad(e)
    {
      if (e.type == "mouseover")
        e.srcElement.style.color="#FF6633"
      else if (e.type == "mouseout")
        e.srcElement.style.color="#006600"
    }
  </script>
</head>
<body>
  <!-- The following anchor has event handlers in it -->
  <p onMouseOver="good(event);"
     onMouseOut="good(event);" >Good Highlight</p>
   <p onMouseOver="bad(event);"
     onMouseOut="bad(event);" >Bad Highlight</p>
</body>
</html>
```

Listing 5.12   Subtle color effects

For the same reason, you should avoid throwing alert messages at your users. An alert message disrupts the user's train of thought and ability to navigate your website. In case a user enters incorrect data or omits a critical field, use the DOM to highlight the field and add a text message rather than forcing the user to hunt down numerous alert pop-ups.

Referencing the Event Object with Different Browsers

The event object is often used in scripting to obtain information about the nature of the event. For example, we could use it to determine the kind of element that triggered the event, or what element is currently servicing the event. However, Netscape and IE each implement different versions of the event interface.

The W3C defines an Event Standard Interface in the DOM Level 2 specification (which is an extension of DOM Level 1. See the appendix to this CodeNote for more information on the different DOM levels). Netscape 6.0 implements an event model that adheres to this standard. IE 5+, on the other hand, implements a non-W3C-compliant Level 2 event model. In Netscape, the event object is automatically passed to a function assigned to an event handler. For example, consider the following:

```
<script>
  click_handler(e)
  {
    alert (e.tagName);
  }

  document.forms[0].button1.onclick = click_handler;
</script>

<input type="button" value="Push Me" />
```

Listing 5.13   An event handler assignment in Netscape (W3C DOM event model)

Netscape will implicitly pass the event as the first argument if you leave the event out of the function call. In other words, you do not have to explicitly pass the event into the method, even though the method defines the event as an argument. IE, on the other hand, defines a global event object, window.event, which effectively eliminates the need for passing the event at all, as illustrated in Listing 5.14.

```
<script>
  //notice, no arguments!
  click_handler()
  {
```

```
  //global event object is window.event
  alert (window.event.tagName);
}
document.forms[0].button1.onclick = click_handler();
</script>

<input type="button" value="Push Me" />
```

Listing 5.14   Event handler in IE

However, the solutions are mutually exclusive. Netscape's notation will not work for IE, and IE's notation will not work for Netscape. A cross-browser solution is to explicitly pass the event at the element level to a handler method that takes an element parameter, as illustrated in Listing 5.15.

```
<script>
  function click_handler(e) {
    alert (e.tagName);
  }
</script>
<input type=button value="Click Me" name="button1" id="button1"
  onclick="click_handler(event)">
```

Listing 5.15   Cross-browser event trapping

Both IE and Netscape will pass the event into the function as a local variable.

Browser Specific Event Methods

Once you have passed the event, you will still need to fork your code to access the event attributes for different browsers, since the event object implementation differs for Netscape and IE. See the compatibility tables in the appendix for a listing of how to handle the different attributes for each browser type. For more on how to fork code based on browser differences, see the topic, "The Document Object Model," later in this chapter.

SUMMARY

Event handlers, when used wisely, can enrich your website. However, event handlers are some of the most abused aspects of DHTML. Always keep the user's experience in mind when you write new event handlers. Does the event handler make the user perform extra mouse clicks? Does the event handler violate the color rules from Chapter 3? Does the event handler block normal functions? If the answer is yes, you probably shouldn't build the function. On the other hand, you should use event handlers for:

1. Creating subtle highlight effects to get the user's attention
2. Launching client-side validation of user data through regular expressions
3. Adding pop-up effects containing more details on a particular web component
4. Other effects that enhance the user experience by removing roadblocks, providing useful information, or automating data entry

Whenever you use an event handler to change color, keep in mind the color rules from Chapter 3.

Topic: Cascading Style Sheets

Cascading Style Sheets (CSS) are another part of DHTML. CSS is simply a way of grouping one or more related elements under the umbrella of a single class. In this way, when you wish to apply the grouping of attributes to a particular element, you can simply use the class name as opposed to repeatedly typing the attributes inside the HTML element. In doing so, you are inherently separating your content logic from your presentation logic.

CSS is a very useful tool for creating high-quality websites. You can use CSS to control basic formatting and color selections, creating a uniform look and feel for every page. You can also change the look and feel simply by changing the CSS. By editing a single CSS file, you can change the look of every page tied to that CSS.

Cascading Style Sheets get their name from the fact that particular attributes are applied sequentially to an HTML element. In other words, if you define a global text font, the font cascades to every element. You can, however, override the font or specific portions of the font definition at a more specific level of the stylesheet. CSS definitions follow a very simple inheritance model.

CONCEPTS

Basic CSS and Class Selectors

To demonstrate the utility of CSS, suppose that important text within <p> elements is always boldfaced and red. If we have many important lines, the resulting HTML looks scattered and has many duplicated tags:

```
<html>
<head>
</head>
<body>
   <P><FONT color=red ><b>This is important.</b>  </FONT>  </P>
   <P>This is not important.</P>
   <P><FONT color=red >
     <b>Oh, this is important.</b>
   </FONT></P>
   <P><FONT color=red ><b>So is this!</b></FONT>  </P>
   <P>This is not.</P>
</body>
</html>
```

Listing 5.16   An HTML document using traditional formatting tags

It would be really nice if we could group the red and bold tags together as a common class (known as a *class selector*) and use the name of the class (let's call it "important") instead of the individual tags. Fortunately, CSS allows us to do just that. Rewriting the previous HTML using CSS we now have:

```
<html>
<style>p.important {color:red; font-weight:bold}</style>
<body>
<P class="important">This is important.</P>
<P>This is not important.</P>
<P class="important">Oh, this is important. </P>
<P class="important">So is this!  </P>
<P>This is not.</P>
</body>
</html>
```

Listing 5.17   Using CSS within an HTML document

The <style> tags in Listing 5.17 create a new CSS class named "important." This class contains both color (red) and font (bold) attributes. We can then apply the "important" class to any <p> element via the attribute class="important".

Class Selector Syntax

The basic syntax for a class selector contains several components:

1. All class selectors are encapsulated in <style> tags. You can actually define multiple styles within a single tag:

```
<style type="text/css">
  * {color:red}
  b {color:yellow; font-weight:bold;}
</style>
```

Listing 5.18   Declaring multiple styles

Because we used the * wildcard, the first style defined in Listing 5.18 will turn all text red, whereas the second definition will only make text inside <b> tags yellow and bold.

2. The first part of the selector optionally identifies an HTML tag type (<p> in Listing 5.17), and provides a name for the class (important in Listing 5.17). Note that, as we have defined it, the "important" class can be used only with <p> elements. If you wanted to make the "important" class available to be associated with any attribute, you could rewrite the <style> line and omit the "p" prefix:

```
.important {color:red; font-weight:bold}
```

Listing 5.19   Making a class available to be associated with any element

The "important" class can now be used with any element (provided, of course, that color and font-weight properties are meaningful to that element).

3. The final part contains attribute definitions. A complete list of CSS attributes can be found at ⊶UI050003. However, several important attributes will be described in the following sections.

Interestingly, it is also possible to apply CSS properties to an element via the element's id as opposed to its type or class. For example, if you had the following HTML element:

```
<b id="special">This text is special</b>
```

Listing 5.20   A simple element with an id attribute

You could give the `special` element a yellow background by placing the following between <style> tags:

```
#special {background:yellow}
```

Listing 5.21   Applying a style to an element with the id "special"

This notation complements the HTML tag identification used in Listing 5.17. Examples of this selector notation and many of the more important attribute types are included throughout this topic.

In-Line CSS Definitions

You can use a third method to define CSS definitions for use in a single, specific element. Simply add a `style` attribute, containing the CSS definition:

```
<b style="background:yellow">This text is special</b>
```

Listing 5.22   In-line CSS definitions

This sort of in-line definition is particularly useful when you need to override a default style for a single element. In particular, you will see this notation used frequently to position HTML elements, as described in the next concept.

CSS Positioning

There are times when you would like to specify exactly where a particular bit of data will be displayed on the client's browser. If all clients had the same screen resolution size and you could be assured that the size of everyone's browser window would always be the same, this would not be a problem. Given, however, that we don't have this luxury, CSS gives us two ways to specify position: absolute and relative. Regardless of the browser's screen dimensions, these two position types can be used to create an appropriate layout.

Absolute Positioning

Absolute positioning allows you to specify where you want the element to appear in the context of the entire window. Absolute positioning can be defined in terms of either pixels or percentages. As we saw in Chapter 3, however, not everyone's window will be the same size or at the same resolution. Therefore, it is better to use percentages if possible.

```
<p style="position:absolute; top:10%; left:50%">Goodbye!</p>
```

Listing 5.23   Using absolute positioning with percentages

In this snippet, the word "Goodbye!" will appear 10 percent of the screen height from the top, and 50 percent of the screen width from the left. If the browser is resized, "Goodbye" will retain its absolute position with regard to the screen size. Pixel notation would replace the percentages with pixel amounts such as 5px (5 pixels). As mentioned in Chapter 3, converting from pixels to percentages or real units (inches) is not very easy and is specific to the particular browser and screen resolution. Listing 5.23, like most CSS positioning elements, was declared in line with the actual HTML element.

Relative Positioning
Relative positioning allows you to specify a position relative to a parent element. As with absolute positioning, you can specify relative position in terms of either pixels or percentages. The following example makes bold text larger than normal text and positions it lower relative to the normal text so that it is centered on the line:

```
<html>
  <head>
    <style type="text/css">
      p {position:absolute; top:20%; left:40%}
      b {position:relative; top:5px;
         font-size:x-large; font-weight:bold;}
    </style>
  </head>
  <body>
    <p>Come to our absolutely <b>HUGE</b> summer sale!!</p>
  </body>
</html>
```

Listing 5.24   Using relative positioning

The result of Listing 5.24 is shown in Figure 5.1.

Come to our absolutely **HUGE** summer sale!!

Figure 5.1   Using relative positioning

Figure 5.2 shows the same text without the relative position styling of the bold element.

Come to our absolutely **HUGE** summer sale!!

Figure 5.2   Without relative positioning

As you can see, relative positioning can be used in conjunction with absolute positioning to create rather complicated layouts that are mostly independent of the user's browser or screen resolution. Try to arrange your web pages so that all of the important content is visible at the lowest anticipated resolution, but that the components automatically scale to the available screen space, using absolute and relative positioning.

CSS in Separate Files

In addition to storing CSS directly in your HTML page, you can create separate CSS files and link the files to multiple pages. So far we have seen CSS used internally; that is, all the CSS classes are defined between <style> elements in an HTML page (e.g., Listing 5.17). It is possible, however, to take all the CSS classes and place them in a separate file—let's call it mysheet.css—and simply reference this external file within the <head> elements of your HTML page:

```
<head>
  <link rel="stylesheet" href="mysheet.css" type="textless">
</head>
```

Listing 5.25   Linking to an external CSS stylesheet

The CSS file, mysheet.css, will not contain any HTML or other syntax; it will simply hold your CSS classes (<style> tag elements are not necessary in CSS files). A simple CSS file might look like Listing 5.26.

```
p.topleft {position:absolute; top:20%; left:40%}
b.vert_centered {position:relative; top:5px;
  font-size:x-large; font-weight:bold;}
```

Listing 5.26   A simple CSS file (mysheet.css)

EXAMPLE

Suppose we have an HTML document that has a couple of headings and a simple table:

```
<html>
<body>
```

```
<h1>My Favorite Teams</h1>
<h2>Of The NFL</h2>
<table>
  <tr><th>Team</th><th>City</th></tr>
  <tr><td>Bills</td><td>Buffalo</td></tr>
  <tr><td>Jets</td><td>New York</td></tr>
  <tr><td>Miami</td><td>Dolphins</td></tr>
</table>
</body>
</html>
```

Listing 5.27   Simple HTML document

We want to apply some visual effects, but we'd like to leave the original HTML untouched as much as possible. We'll link to an external stylesheet, which contains some color and positioning effects that we've already discussed:

```
body {background-color:#EEEEFF; color:black;}

h1 {font:small-caps; font-family: Times ; font-size: 25pt;
    color:seagreen; font-style:oblique }
h2 {font-family: Arial Black; font-size: 16pt;
    color:seagreen;}

th {background-color:blue; color:white;
    border-style: ridge; }

table {border:1; width:400px; border-style: ridge;
       vertical-align: middle;}

td {text-align:center; width:200px;
    font-family:tahoma,sans-serif;
    font-size: 12px; border-style: inset;}

.rowdark  {background-color:turquoise;
           text-align:center;
           width:100px;}
```

Listing 5.28   CSS sample file

We are applying color and font effects to the headings, as well as styling effects to the table. We have also defined a new class rowdark, which we have applied to one of the rows in the table. To do this we need to change just one line in the original HTML from Listing 5.27, as well as link to the stylesheet itself.

```
<!--add this line to the top of Listing 5.27 just after the
<html> tag -->
<link rel="stylesheet" href="sample.css">

<!-- Modify the third table row in Listing 5.27, by adding the
class attribute -->
<tr class="rowdark"><td>Jets</td><td>New York</td></tr>
```

Listing 5.29   Modified HTML

Figure 5.3 shows the HTML before and after the application of CSS.

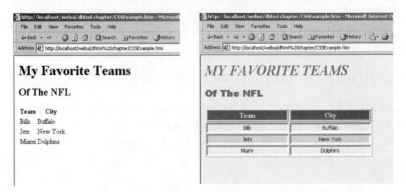

Figure 5.3   Application of CSS using an external file

HOW AND WHY

Why Would I Define My CSS Classes in a Separate File Instead of Using CSS Internally?

The use of external CSS files requires two round-trips for the browser: one to get the HTML file and another to retrieve the associated CSS file. For this reason, it is often advantageous for small websites to declare CSS inside of the HTML pages. However, if you have a very large website serviced by many developers, it can be very convenient to have all your established stylistic conventions in one single stylesheet. In fact, many large corporations dictate color schemes and web look and feel through a standard set of corporation wide CSS files.

BUGS AND CAVEATS

Browser Differences
As is the case with almost all web technology, each major browser supports a different subset of the CSS specification. Because of this, you should test all of your pages on all the browsers your clients could potentially use. See the appendix to this CodeNote for compatibility details.

DESIGN NOTES

Using CSS with JavaScript
You can leverage the style property of an element with JavaScript and, as we will see in the next section, manipulate the property even after a page has loaded. Both Netscape and IE give your JavaScript write privileges to all style attributes defined in a CSS document.

However, most of the CSS1 specification (incorporated in Netscape 6.0 and IE 5+) uses hyphenated words (for example, `border-align`, `background-color`). JavaScript does not allow hyphenated words as identifiers. All CSS properties are therefore converted to an interCap notation when using JavaScript. This notation removes the hyphen and capitalizes the second word. Keeping with the previous example, `border-align` would be accessed as `style.borderAlign`, whereas `background-color` would be `style.backgroundColor`. Keep this convention in mind when you are using JavaScript to access CSS properties.

SUMMARY

Cascading Style Sheets are one of the most widely used portions of DHTML. CSS gives you the power of separating common format elements into simple definitions. These definitions can be applied to any HTML element in one of four ways:

1. You can create a `<style>` element defining a style class (e.g., `<style>.mystyle {text-align:left}</style>`) for a particular type of HTML element or for general uses by different types of elements. When you insert an HTML element, you can use the `class` attribute (`class="mystyle"`).
2. The HTML element may include an in-line style definition using the style attribute (e.g., `style="text-align:left"`).

3. The HTML element may have an id attribute that matches a particular CSS style definition. In this case, the style will automatically be applied to the HTML element.
4. The CSS file (or <style> tags) may contain default settings for particular types of elements. You could, for example, assign a color set to every <p> tag.

By using CSS, you can create a comprehensive look and feel that applies throughout your website.

Topic: The Document Object Model

The W3C defines DOM as a "platform- and language-neutral interface," allowing programs and scripts to dynamically update HTML document content on the client. Basically, the DOM dictates the manner in which a browser makes the components of a page (elements and their data) available to be read and modified via a language such as JavaScript. Toward this end, the DOM defines a hierarchy of related objects such as documents, windows, links, images, and forms that are programmatically accessible via JavaScript.

The W3C formally defined the DOM Level 1 specification in 1998. In recent years, this specification has been updated several times, and the most recent specification is DOM Level 3. However, Netscape 6.0 and IE 5.5 and above support DOM Level 1, but do not fully support the latest W3C standards (Levels 2 and 3). Prior to version 5.5 of IE and 6 of Netscape, the browsers used proprietary DOMs that were similar, but not fully compatible.

In this topic we will concern ourselves with the DOM Level 1 specification supported by the latest generation of browsers. If you need to target older browsers, the appendix to this CodeNote will outline some of the differences between the older non-W3C DOMs.

CONCEPTS

Basic DOM
The basic DOM hierarchy used by modern browsers looks like Figure 5.4. The DOM window object can be thought of as a browser instance. You can use this top-level object to control web browser instances, including creating new pop-up browsers, as illustrated in Listing 5.30.

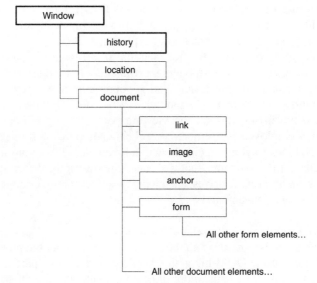

Figure 5.4   The DOM hierarchy

```
<script>
//First arg is the URL, second is the name of the new window
//for use as the target of dynamic links or forms
   NewWindow=window.open("","");
</script>
```

Listing 5.30   Creating a new window

A new instance of your browser will appear containing a blank page. We can now use the document object of the new window (every window and frame has its own document object) from the parent window to manipulate the content of the new window dynamically (Listing 5.31).

```
<script>
   NewWindow=window.open("","");
   NewWindow.document.write("<html><body><p>I am " +
            "in a new window!</p></body></html>");

   // Optional: use the window's moveBy() function
   // to move the window left 50 pixels, and
   // down 50 pixels
   NewWindow.moveBy(-50,50);

</script>
```

Listing 5.31   Manipulating a different window

When run, Listing 5.31 will create a new HTML page and dynamically add contents to it. We are now going to use this technique of new windows/dynamic HTML creation to explore the DOM.

Before you move on to the next section, recall from Chapter 3 that we should refrain from introducing extraneous, redundant, or focus-changing elements to our design. Sadly, popping up new browser windows in this fashion is rarely a good idea. When not being used to force unwanted advertisements on the viewing party, pop-up windows are sometimes employed as a remote-control navigation menu. If this seems like a good idea to you, imagine how much you would like your file explorer on your PC to operate that way: one window for the drives and another for the files on the drives, each window sometimes overlapping the other. Not very convenient, is it?

Using DOM for Common Development Tasks

There are a number of texts and references that will list all the properties and methods of the DOM hierarchy. While you can find a partial list at ⟨CN⟩UI050004, it is, perhaps, more illustrative to explore the DOM from the perspective of common tasks that a developer would want to perform. The solution to these tasks will be the subject of the following sections.

Iterating through HTML Elements of a Document

The document object is, perhaps, the most frequently used object in the DOM. The document can be thought of as the gateway through which you can access all elements of the HTML page; these child elements are kept in the document's childNodes array. Every childNode in the childNodes array supports properties such as firstChild, lastChild, nextSibling, and previousSibling, which can be used to iterate through the elements of your page. Listing 5.32 illustrates how to use the properties of childNode to recursively display all elements of a particular page or document in a tree.

```html
<html>
<head><script>
  var outputStr = new String();
  var level;
  outputStr = ""; level = 0;

  function iterateTree()
  {
    // This function iterates through the entire DOM hierarchy
    // Start off at the top
    showTree(document.childNodes[0]);
```

```
    document.write(outputStr);
  }

  function showTree(currentNode)
  {
    var currentChild;

    // Display our current node if it's a valid element
    if (currentNode.tagName)
      displayTag(currentNode)

    // Iterate to the next node
    currentChild = currentNode.firstChild;
    while (currentChild)
    {
      level++;
      //recursive call
      showTree(currentChild);
      currentChild = currentChild.nextSibling;
    }
    level--;
  }
  function displayTag(currentNode)
  {
    outputStr += "<img src='spacer.gif' "+
      "height=0 width=" + (level*20) + ">";
    outputStr += "<font style='color:red'>"
    outputStr += currentNode.tagName;
    outputStr += "</font><font style='color:blue'> "
    outputStr += currentNode.id;
    outputStr +="</font><font style='color:black'> "
    outputStr += "</font><BR>";
  }
</script></head>
<body><form>
<input type="button" width=100 name="Tree" id="Tree"
    value="Tree" onclick="iterateTree()">
</form></body>
</html>
```

Listing 5.32 showtree.html

In this particular example, the document contains <head>, <title>, <script>, and <body> elements. The <body> element contains an

<input> element, named "Tree". See ⊶UI050005 for more detailed examples, including some IE-specific navigation techniques.

Retrieving a Particular HTML Element by ID

If you wish to get a reference to a particular element in your HTML you can always iterate through every element as shown in the previous section. However, you can also use document.getElementById() to get an element directly, assuming the element has an id attribute. For example, if we create a text box in HTML like so:

```
<input id="uid" type="text" name="T1" size="20"></p>
```

Listing 5.33   A simple input element with an id attribute

we can retrieve a reference to this text box from JavaScript (perhaps to perform validation on the value entered) by using code similar to the following:

```
alert( document.getElementById("uid").value );
```

Listing 5.34   Using the getElementByID function

This method will work as long as the id element is unique. If the element ID is not unique, the behavior is not defined. In other words, the script may return any of the elements with a matching id, or it may return an error. If an invalid id is specified (i.e., one that does not exist), the method will return null.

Retrieving HTML Element Groups by Type

If you would like to retrieve a reference to all elements of a given type, as opposed to one particular instance, you can use document.getElementsByTagName(). This method returns an array of all elements of a particular type. If, for example, you wanted to retrieve and iterate through all of the <p> elements in your HTML page, you could simply use the following:

```
<html>
<head>
  <script>
    x=document.getElementsByTagName("p");
    for(i=0; i<x.length; i++)
    {
      //do something with object
    }
```

```
  </script>
</head>
<body>
  <p>One</p>
  <p>Two</p>
</body>
</html>
```

Listing 5.35   Retrieving all <p> elements with the getElementsByTagName function

If we were looking at a more generic tag type, such as <input>, we would have to use a specific check inside of the for loop to look for the specific variant (e.g., a text input).

Changing Raw HTML Dynamically

Using the DOM, it is possible to read and modify HTML dynamically. When retrieved as objects (perhaps via getElementById()) all HTML elements will have the following properties: innerHTML, outerHTML, innerText, and outerText. These properties give us an enormous amount of real-time control over our page, allowing us to change the HTML and content of a particular tag.

- innerHTML   This property includes the rendered text and HTML tags between the start and end tags of the current element.
- innerText   This property returns the rendered text of the current element. In other words, any HTML included inside of the tag is applied before the text is returned.
- outerHTML   This property returns the entire set of information associated with a tag. The start tag, text, and end tag will be returned. Any child tags inside of the main tag will also be returned. In other words, outerHTML is equivalent to looking at raw HTML code.
- outerText   This property is roughly equivalent to outerHTML, except that all HTML tags are rendered prior to returning the text.

Note that innerText and outerText return the same value. The difference between these two properties is apparent only when you change content. The innerText simply replaces the text between the element tags. The outerText property actually wipes out the entire element, tags and all, and replaces it with text.

Using these properties, Listing 5.36 demonstrates how to change the caption of an element dynamically.

```
<html>
  <body>
    <script>
      function changeit() {
        document.getElementById("mytext").innerText="Goodbye!";
      }
    </script>
    <p id="mytext">Hello!</p>
    <form><input type="button" value="Say Goodbye"
                  onClick="changeit();">
    </form>
  </body>
</html>
```

Listing 5.36   Using innerText to change element content

While innerText and outerText are useful, innerHTML and outerHTML are awesomely powerful. With innerHTML and outerHTML you can change the fundamental structure of the HTML page dynamically. For example, you could add a form, change styles of elements, and create or destroy tables. Anything you can do when first creating a page in a text editor, you can do in JavaScript after the page is already rendered. In general, if an element has an id tag, you can retrieve it and use inner/outerHTML to change it to any HTML you would like.

In Listing 5.37, we have a simple button entitled "Add Link." When pressed, it will call our AddLink() function, which will prompt the user for a URL via JavaScript's prompt() function. The prompt() function displays a message box that solicits a string value from the user. When the user enters the URL and clicks OK, AddLink() uses outerHTML to dynamically construct a proper <a href> link and add it to the bottom of the page.

```
<html>
<head>
</head>
<body>
<p> My Links: </p>
<div id="Holder"></div>
<input type="button" value="Add Link" onClick="AddLink()"></p>
</body>
<script>
  function AddLink()
  {
    v=document.getElementById("Holder");
```

```
        s=prompt("Give me a URL:");
        old=v.innerHTML;
        s="<p><a href=http://"+s+">"+s+"</a></p>"+old;
        v.innerHTML=s;
    }
</script>
</html>
```

Listing 5.37   Adding a link dynamically

If you try this example, you should see a new href link after you click
on the Add Link button and enter a URL.

Browser Differences
Unfortunately, IE and Netscape differ on the implementation of these
properties. Netscape in particular implements only the innerHTML property in version 6.0 (see Design Notes). However, we can still use this
property to dynamically examine and change the nodes within the
DOM.

   If you recall from the previous section entitled "Iterating through
HTML Elements of a Document," we can iterate through all the
elements of an HTML page starting from the childNodes property of
the document object. All node objects support a method named
appendChild(); thus, it is always possible to append a new node to an
existing one (or remove one, for that matter).

   An easier method involves retrieving a specific node using the
document.getElementById() method and then calling appendChild() on
the returned node. This is shown in Listing 5.38.

```
<html>
<p id="p1"> The Secret to life is...<p>
<script>
  function addChild(node, elementName, id, content)
  {
    var n;
    n = document.createElement(elementName);
    n.id = id;
    n.innerHTML = content;
    node.appendChild(n);
  }
  var x;
  x=document.getElementById("p1");
  addChild(x, "B", "newNode",
    "something I will <i>never</i> share.");
```

```
</script>
<html>
```

Listing 5.38   Appending a child element

The resulting HTML page of Listing 5.31 is shown in Figure 5.5.

The Secret to life is... **something I will *never* share.**

Figure 5.5   The secret of life

As you can see, the second half of the statement was added through JavaScript. You can use this technique to add, delete, or alter any HTML elements on the page.

EXAMPLE

We can use what we've learned to generate a simple dynamic form. Suppose we want users to enter some information dynamically, but we want to let them choose the way they can enter it. We'll give them two different methods of data entry. They can choose from Option A (a simple text box where they can enter their name) or Option B (a combination text box and combo box, where the combo box already has some sample last names in it—they can find their name in the box). In this example we've only filled the combo box with three names.

The code for this uses concepts we've already discussed—namely, appending a node to the DOM tree and the innerHTML property of an element.

```
<html>
<head>

<script language="javascript">
function setForm(formType)
{
  var str = new String();
  var obj;

  str = "First<input type='text'><br>Last"

  switch(formType)
  {
```

```
    case('a'):
      str += "<input type='text'>"
      break;
    case('b'):
      str += "<select><option selected>Orr</option>";
      str += "<option>Howe</option>";
      str += "<option>LeFleur</option></select>";
      break;
  }
  obj = document.createElement('div');
  obj.innerHTML = str;
  document.getElementById('rootDiv').appendChild(obj);
}
</script>

</head>
<body>
<form>
  <h1>Input your Name</h1>
  <input type="button" value="Option A" onclick="setForm('a')">
  <input type="button" value="Option B" onclick="setForm('b')">
  <p>Click one of the two options to enter your name</p>
  <div id="rootDiv"></div>
</form>
</body>
</html>
```

Listing 5.39   Creating a dynamic form

The JavaScript function setForm takes in a parameter a or b, depending on what option the user has clicked. We then build a string that we will stuff inside a <div> tag that we create dynamically using the DOM method createMethod. We fill this <div> tag with the appropriate string using its innerHTML property. Finally, we add the element to the DOM tree with the method appendChild.

Figure 5.6 shows the result if the user had clicked on Option B.

HOW AND WHY

How Do I Enable or Disable Input Tags in My Forms?

Using the DOM, you can enable or disable <input> elements in your forms by changing the disabled attribute. An example of when you

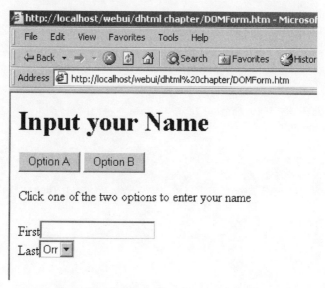

Figure 5.6   Creating a dynamic name entry system

would use this is in a form where the user chooses a payment method. If the user were to choose to pay by cash on delivery, you would disable the text field for the credit card information (in Listing 5.40, we assume this field is called creditcardtext). This can be done by including the following line in the function that handles your onClick event for choosing cash on delivery.

```
document.getElementById("creditcardtext").disabled="true";
```

Listing 5.40   Disabling an input field

Once you have disabled an input element, you can enable it by simply setting the disabled attribute to false.

DESIGN NOTES

InnerHTML across Browsers

You should by this time be aware that there are a significant number of DHTML properties available that are not part of the W3C DOM. Both Netscape and IE have implemented custom properties that are not standardized, but are incorporated because they add a significant amount of DHTML value. Microsoft, for example, defined their innerHTML attribute in IE 4+, which has since been incorporated by Netscape in their version 6.0 browser. Because it is so easy to use (as opposed to dynamically adding or removing nodes from the DOM), designers commonly use this attribute to modify a portion of a page's content after the page has loaded.

However, of the four attributes mentioned in this CodeNote (outerHTML, outerText, innerText, innerHTML), Netscape 6.0 supports only innerHTML. Netscape 4.x and earlier do not support innerHTML at all. Be aware, when designing your web page, that the use of outerHTML, outerText, and innerText (and innerHTML in any Netscape browser version older than 6.x) will make your page unusable in a Netscape browser.

Using the Navigator Property for Browser Detection

There will often be times in your script when you would like to know the browser type and version that is running your code. You may, for example, want to fork your code so you can use each browser's DOM correctly. To do this, you can use the navigator object, which is contained within the top-level window object.

The navigator object has four core properties: appCodeName, appName, appVersion, and userAgent. We can use the appName to distinguish between Netscape and IE:

```
<script language="javascript">
  document.write(window.navigator.appName);
</script>
```

Listing 5.41   Determining browser version

The resulting output would be "Netscape" for Netscape, and "Microsoft Internet Explorer" for IE.

You can use this property in a conditional statement to make your code browser-specific. However, at times we'd also like to know the version number of the browser we're using (Netscape's 4.x is vastly different from 6.0, for example). Determining version is actually a bit trickier. We can use the appVersion attribute, but we need to parse the output:

```
document.write(window.navigator.appVersion);
```

Listing 5.42   Determining browser version

When this code fragment runs on IE 5.5, for example, it produces an output of "*4.0 (compatible; MSIE 5.5; Windows NT 5.0; COM | 1.0.2204; .NET CLR 1.0.2914).*"

Note that the first number in the string doesn't necessarily represent the specific browser version, but, rather, a broad generation number.

Specifically, this tells us that all the features of IE 4.0 are supported in this particular version (IE 5.5). However, if we require the real version number, we can extract it using the JavaScript built-in string function indexOf. This method will return a value of −1 if it does not find a character match:

```
if (parseInt(window.navigator.appVersion)) > 4)
{
  // Code fork for IE 4+
}
If (window.navigator.appVersion.indexOf("MSIE 5") != -1)
{
  // Code fork for IE 5.5
}
```

Listing 5.43   Using indexOf to extract version

Fortunately, a similar approach can be used for extracting Netscape versions. The appVersion command generates the following strings for Netscape:

- Netscape 4.7, on Windows 2000—"4.7 [en] (WinNT; I)"
- Netscape 6.0, on Windows 2000—"- 5.0 (Windows; en-US)"

Simply look for the indexOf "4." or "5.".

SUMMARY

The DOM provides a set of tools that can be used to link your JavaScript code to the actual HTML content of a page. By combining the DOM with JavaScript, you can modify any HTML element, add new elements, or delete existing elements, all on the client's browser.

Like event handlers, however, the DOM can be abused. If you recall from Chapter 3, blocking common functionality, such as the Back button, can create an unfriendly web experience. Make sure that you leave these common functions intact. Do not resize the browser or create unnecessary pop-up windows. Do not prevent users from closing the page or block access to common features such as printing. These features are expected by your users and should be left in place.

Chapter Summary

Event handlers, CSS, and the DOM provide the core features for client-side web-based user interfaces. It is very difficult to develop a compelling website without taking advantage of event handling, standard look-and-feel elements, or the event hooks provided by the DOM.

All three of these technologies, however, are somewhat browser-specific. The appendix to this CodeNote includes a comprehensive list of many of these differences. However, you should always test your DHTML effects on your targeted browsers.

Chapter 6

XML/XSLT

Extensible Markup Language (XML) is a globally accepted, browser-independent standard for representing data. XML provides a simple medium for storing and transporting hierarchical data. In order for a browser to display XML content in an attractive or functional manner, however, you will want to convert the data to HTML. The Extensible Stylesheet Language Transformation (XSLT) standard provides an XML-based framework for transforming an XML document into another form such as HTML. Through the use of XSLT, you can separate your data (XML) from your presentation (HTML) and easily convert your data into a graphical format. This chapter covers the most commonly used aspects of XML and XSLT with user interfaces. For a more in-depth discussion of XML and XSLT, including DTDs and XML schemas, please see *CodeNotes for XML*.

Before continuing with this chapter, it is recommended that you have an XSLT processor that can take an XML file, process it through an XSL file, and transform it to HTML. See Chapter 2 for more instructions on installing browsers and our recommended XSLT processor (SAXON).

SIMPLE APPLICATION

In this example, we will transform a simple XML document into an HTML document. Listing 6.1 is an XML file representing a simple greeting that we will display in HTML format. Save the text in Listing 6.1 as `greeting.xml`.

```
<?xml version="1.0"?>
<greeting>What's up, Doc?</greeting>
```

Listing 6.1   greeting.xml

The "xml" extension is not mandatory. However, it is standard practice to save generic XML files with this prefix.

The rules for transforming greeting.xml into an HTML document are stored in the XSLT file shown in Listing 6.2. You will notice that both greeting.xml and transform.xsl have a similar file structure. This similarity is due to the fact that both documents are, in fact, XML documents; transform.xsl is simply a specialized XML document containing rules for transforming another XML document.

```
<?xml version="1.0"?>
<xsl:stylesheet version="1.0"
    xmlns:xsl="http://www.w3.org/1999/XSL/Transform">
<xsl:output method="html"/>

<!-- one rule - transform the root of the input XML document -->
<xsl:template match="/">
  <html>
  <head><title>Hello World!</title></head>
  <body><h1><xsl:value-of select="greeting"/></h1></body>
  </html>
</xsl:template>

</xsl:stylesheet>
```

Listing 6.2   transform.xsl

XSLT files are generally saved with the "xsl" extension; however, this rule is not mandatory. Depending on the XSL processor you are using, you will follow different steps to transform the XML document.

Full Saxon (Java application)
If you are a Java developer, ensure that saxon.jar is in your CLASSPATH and run:

```
java com.icl.saxon.StyleSheet greeting.xml
transform.xsl-a simple.xml
```

Listing 6.3   Using SAXON to transform an XML document

Instant Saxon (Windows Executable)
Ensure that the directory containing saxon.exe is in your PATH variable and from a command prompt run:

```
saxon -O simple.xml greeting.xml transform.xsl
```

Listing 6.4   Using Instant Saxon to transform an XML document

Regardless of the manner you used to transform the XML document, you should receive output similar to Listing 6.5.

```
<html>
  <head>
    <title>Hello World!</title>
  </head>
  <body>
    <h1>What's up, doc?</h1>
  </body>
</html>
```

Listing 6.5   simple.html

Notice that the raw XML from Listing 6.1 is now transformed into a standard HTML document that can be displayed in any browser. Later in this chapter, you will learn how to perform this transformation inside of a web browser.

CORE CONCEPTS

Separating Data from Presentation
By using XML and XSLT, you can store the information to be displayed in one document (the XML file) and the rules for displaying the information in a different file (the XSLT stylesheet file). This makes it very easy to change either the data or the presentation without affecting the other part. When the data and its presentation are combined in a single file (as is the case with normal HTML files), it can be quite difficult to ensure that a change to the data does not affect the presentation, and vice versa.

Topic: XML

Ordinary HTML documents store web content in a simple text file, where the data and display information are intermixed. XML documents, on the other hand, are used to store structured information of any type. Both HTML and XML files contain elements and attributes to describe the information contained within the document. HTML documents, however, are restricted to a particular set of tags and structure, whereas the elements of XML documents are specified entirely by the author. In an XML document, you can create your own tags and structure.

An XML document must follow a fairly strict set of rules to be valid or well-formed. As you will see in the following concepts, the rules for a well-formed XML document are similar to, but much stricter than, the rules for a valid HTML document.

CONCEPTS

Elements
XML elements are very similar to HTML elements; there are, however, a few subtle differences. The most noticeable difference is that XML elements can have any name. In HTML, there is a standard set of tags that you may use that browsers are hard-wired to understand, such as <table>, <p>, and <head>. However, in XML, you are free to use any element names that you think correctly describe your data. For example, Listing 6.6 is a valid XML document describing the residents of a house.

```
<?xml version="1.0"?>
<house>
   <occupant>Mark Fellin</occupant>
   <occupant>Paul Armstrong</occupant>
   <occupant>Mike Van Atter</occupant>
   <occupant>Erin Peterson</occupant>
</house>
```

Listing 6.6   house.xml

Another way that XML elements are different from HTML elements is that XML elements are case-sensitive. In HTML a <P> element is the same as a <p> element, whereas in XML these tags would be treated as different elements.

Start and End Tags
Every element in an XML document must have a start tag and an end tag. Open-ended HTML elements such as
 (line break) cannot exist legally in XML, although <br/> can, since it uses XML's empty element

syntax (demonstrated in Listing 6.8). As a side note, many browsers will accept the <br /> notation in HTML, add a line break, and simply ignore the extra "/" character.

The following is a well-formed XML fragment consisting of a start tag, some data, and an end tag:

```
<text>Some text here</text>
```

Listing 6.7   A valid XML element

As mentioned previously, to create an empty tag in XML, you must add the "/" character to the end of the start tag:

```
<empty_element />
```

Listing 6.8   An empty element

An empty tag cannot contain either character data or child elements.

No Overlapping Elements
XML elements cannot overlap. That is, the closing tag of a child element nested within a parent must appear before the closing tag of the parent element.

```
<para>This
  <ital>fragment</ital>
  is
  <bold>well-formed XML</bold>.
</para>
```

Listing 6.9   Well-formed nested elements

This rule does not exist in HTML, where it is perfectly legal, for example, to have <i> tags that cross <b> tags:

```
<p>This
  fragment
  <i>is
  <b>not well-formed </i>
  xml, although it is legal HTML
  </b>
<p>
```

Listing 6.10   Valid HTML, but invalid XML

In order to convert this listing to proper XML, you would have to add </i> after "is" and insert an <i> tag after the <b> tag.

Root Element

Every XML document must have exactly one root element. Documents without a root element, or with multiple root elements, are not well-formed. In XML the root element can be any legal element name, whereas in HTML the root element is always `<html>`.

The following fragment is a well-formed, fully complete XML document:

```
<?xml version="1.0?>
<rootElement>
  <childElement>Child 1</childElement>
  <childElement>Another child</childElement>
</rootElement>
```

Listing 6.11   A well-formed XML document

Every element contained in the document is automatically a child of the root element.

Attributes

Like HTML tags, XML tags may contain attributes. An attribute is simply a name-value pair inserted in the open-tag definition. Attribute names are case-sensitive, and attribute values must be enclosed in either single or double quotation marks. In HTML, it is legal (although not recommended) to have attribute values that are not enclosed in quotation marks. As with HTML attributes, XML attribute names must also be unique within a particular element. For example, Listing 6.12 illustrates an element tag with two attributes:

```
<element att1="value1" att2="value2"/>
```

Listing 6.12   Well-formed attributes

Attribute values cannot contain, as printable characters, the same quotes with which they have been delimited. For example, consider Listing 6.13, which encapsulates double quotes inside an attribute.

```
<!-- version 1 -->
<address quote='"Four score and seven years..."' />
<!-- version 2, using entity references -->
<address quote = "&quot;Four score and seven years...&quot;"
```

Listing 6.13   Nesting quotation marks

The second version uses special character equivalents for the double quote (&quot), called *entity references,* which are discussed in the next section.

Illegal Characters and Entity References

As with HTML, character data in XML documents cannot contain "<" or "&." These characters have a recognized function in XML markup and are therefore reserved. If you want these characters to appear in your text, you must replace them with entity references. XML defines five entity references to provide escape sequences for the reserved characters, all having the general form &referencename;, as listed in Table 6.1.

Reserved Character	Entity Reference
<	&lt;
>	&gt;
"	&quot;
'	&apos;
&	&amp;

Table 6.1   XML entity references

You can use these entity references in any data text inside an XML document, including attribute values and character data between tags.

XML Declaration

The XML declaration is used to identify a document as an XML document. If included, the declaration must appear as the first line of an XML document. While the XML declaration is not strictly required, it should be included. A typical XML declaration looks like this:

```
<?xml version="1.0" encoding="UTF-16"?>
```

Listing 6.14   Sample XML declaration

As the XML standard is case-sensitive, all attributes (version and encoding), as well as the element name (xml), must be lowercase.

The version attribute must always be included in the XML declaration and will always contain the value "1.0" (at least until a new XML standard is released). The encoding attribute is optional, but all attributes must appear in the order shown.

The optional encoding attribute is used to tell the application reading the XML how the text in your XML document is encoded. The value for this attribute depends on the manner in which your system encodes text; but the standard settings are either UTF-8 (ASCII-like 1-3-byte encoding) or UTF-16 (Unicode—2 bytes per character), either of which will work under most circumstances.

Namespaces

XML namespaces allow you to further divide your structured data into application-specific groups. In the discussion on XSLT, we will see how namespaces are used by programs reading an XML document.

Another advantage of namespaces is that they help to eliminate name collisions. A collision could occur if, for example, you had a <name> element describing franchise names (e.g., "McDonald's on Broadway"), and another <name> element describing employee names (e.g., "Ryan Bayley") in the same XML document. An application reading this XML could become confused because the same tag element is used to describe two entirely different sets of data.

Uniqueness

Since namespaces exist to remove ambiguity, it makes sense that namespace names must, themselves, be unique. Because of this, namespaces are identified by a unique Uniform Resource Indicator, or *URI*. Note that URI should not be confused with URL (Uniform Resource Locator), which is actually a *type* of URI, commonly identified by the HTTP protocol. Although most people do use URLs to identify namespaces, the URI can be any string. URLs or URL derivatives are commonly used because a URL is registered and is therefore unique to a particular company or organization, whereas an arbitrary string has no such protection.

Declaring and Using Namespaces

XML namespaces can be declared in any element within an XML document, using the reserved attribute prefix xmlns, as illustrated in Listing 6.15. A namespace will apply only to the children of the element in which it is declared as well as the element itself. In other words, if you want a global namespace, you must add it to the XML root element.

Once a namespace has been declared you can specify that an element or attribute belongs to that namespace by affixing the element or attribute with a prefix representing the namespace. For example, <players:captain> would refer to the <captain> element in the players namespace.

The example in Listing 6.15 declares and uses two namespaces: "www.codenotes.com/players," which uses the prefix players, and "www.codenotes.com/team," which uses the prefix team.

```
<roster xmlns:team="www.codenotes.com/team"
    xmlns:players="www.codenotes.com/players">
  <team:NHL team:name="Toronto Maple Leafs">
    <players:captain players:name="Mats Sundin"/>
```

```
  <players:assistant players:name="Dmitri Yushkevich"/>
  <players:assistant players:name="Gary Roberts"/>
  </team:NHL>
</roster>
```

Listing 6.15   An XML fragment using two namespaces—players and team

It is important to note, however, that roster is neither in the team namespace nor in the players namespace. For roster to be included in either namespace it would have to be appropriately prefixed. To clarify, examine the following namespace declarations:

```
1.   <author xmlns:aut="http://www.authors.org/namespace">
2.   <aut:author xmlns:aut="http://www.authors.org/namespace">
```

Listing 6.16   Two namespace declarations

1. Defines a new namespace, but author is not associated with the namespace.
2. Same as above, but the author element is associated with the namespace. Note that its descendants still need to be explicitly prefixed with aut to be associated with the namespace.

In other words, the tag that defines the namespace is not automatically included in the namespace.

EXAMPLE

Using XML to Store Band Information

The example in Listing 6.17 is a simple XML file containing a band element with child elements for each band member.

```
<?xml version="1.0"?>
<bands>
  <band name="The Who">
    <genre>Rock &amp; Roll</genre>
    <member firstName="Pete" lastName="Townshend">
      <instrument>Guitar</instrument>
    </member>
    <member firstName="Roger" lastName="Daltrey">
      <instrument>Vocals</instrument>
    </member>
```

```
  <member firstName="John" lastName="Entwhistle">
    <instrument>Bass</instrument>
  </member>
  <member firstName="Keith" lastName="Moon">
    <instrument>Drums</instrument>
    <replacement firstName="Kenney" lastName="Jones"/>
  </member>
 </band>
</bands>
```

Listing 6.17   thewho.xml

Most XML documents follow a similar pattern, with a simple container root element and one or more significant child elements. This example could easily be expanded to include other bands by simply adding more <band> tags inside of the root element.

Namespaces Example

In this example, we use the MathML namespace to represent a mathematical equation. The MathML namespace is defined by the W3C (World Wide Web Consortium) and is used to store the contents of mathematical equations for display on the Web. In Listing 6.18, we store the equation 2 times 2 equals 4.

```
<?xml version="1.0"?>
<equation>
  <m:math xmlns:m="http://www.w3.org/1998/Math/MathML">
    <m:mrow>
      <m:mrow>
        <m:mn>2</m:mn>
        <m:times/>
        <m:mn>2</m:mn>
      </m:mrow>
      <m:mo>=</m:mo>
      <m:mn>4</m:mn>
    </m:mrow>
  </m:math>
</equation>
```

Listing 6.18   equation.xml

HOW AND WHY

How Do I Place Comments in My XML Document?

XML comments follow the same syntax as HTML comments. That is, they begin with `<!--` and end with `-->`. As with HTML comments, XML comments can span a fraction of a line, a single line, or multiple lines. A sample comment is shown in Listing 6.19.

```
<!-- This is a comment -->
```

Listing 6.19   An XML comment

How Do I Declare a Default Namespace?

It is possible to associate elements and attributes with a namespace without using a prefix by defining a default namespace. As with all namespaces, the default namespace will apply only to child elements of the parent declaring the namespace. However, the default namespace automatically applies to the declaring element. In the following example, `<parentElement>` and all child elements of the `<parentElement>` element are in the www.codenotes.com/team namespace.

```
<parentElement xmlns="www.codenotes.com/team">
  <childElement>Greg</childElement>
  <childElement>Craig</childElement>
  <childElement>Dave</childElement>
  <childElement>Mike</childElement>
  <childElement>Rob</childElement>
</parentElement>
```

Listing 6.20   Declaring a default namespace

DESIGN NOTES

Elements versus Attributes

There is no set rule for when you should use an attribute to store data instead of using an element to store information. Many people feel that attributes are unnecessary (everything can simply be stored as a child element) and are simply a redundant feature in XML. Others believe that attributes can be used to store information that most humans and applications won't need, in order to make the XML file "look better" without removing the information altogether. In the end, the choice of elements versus attributes is simply a choice of aesthetics.

SUMMARY

XML is a simple markup language intended to provide a platform-independent means of maintaining and transporting tree-structured textual data. Like HTML, XML documents consist primarily of elements (start and end tags) and attributes (name-value pairs) containing character data. XML has stricter rules regarding document structure, although only a few simple rules need to be followed for a document to be well-formed. Namespaces in XML documents allow division of XML markup into application-specific blocks.

Topic: XSLT Templates and Matching

Extensible Stylesheet Language Transformation (XSLT) is used to transform an XML document into another form or format. In this topic, we will limit discussion to the transformation of XML into HTML. For a more thorough review of XSLT, see *CodeNotes for XML.*

Two files are involved in an XSLT transformation: the source XML document, which will be transformed, and the XSLT stylesheet document, which defines the transformation rules. These two documents will produce an output document containing data from the source document formatted according to the rules defined in the stylesheet.

CONCEPTS

The XSLT Namespace
In the previous discussion on XML, we mentioned that namespaces are used to organize your data into application-specific groups. For all XSLT documents, elements in the XSLT namespace xsl tell XSLT processors how to transform your XML documents. The XSLT namespace is http://www.w3.org/1999/XSL/Transform and is usually assigned to a prefix of xsl.

Every XSLT document must start with the stylesheet element and XSLT namespace definition, as shown in Listing 6.21.

```
<xsl:stylesheet version="1.0"
    xmlns:xsl="http://www.w3.org/1999/XSL/Transform">
  <!-- Add contents of the stylesheet here -->
</xsl:stylesheet>
```

Listing 6.21   The root element of an XSLT stylesheet

The xsl:stylesheet root element simply tells the XSL processor that the current XML document will contain the rules for transforming an XML document. In other words, this XML document is, in fact, an XSL document (remember that XSL is, itself, a special kind of XML document).

Generating HTML Output

The XSLT processor can generate many different kinds of output, particularly XML and HTML. As discussed in the previous topic, "XML," there are subtle differences between XML syntax and HTML syntax; therefore, we need to tell the XSLT processor to use HTML mode. The xsl:output command is used to tell the XSLT processor which type of output to generate. To specify that the XSLT processor should produce HTML as output, you must include the method="html" attribute in an xsl:output element as is shown in Listing 6.22..

```
<?xml version="1.0"?>
<xsl:stylesheet version="1.0"
    xmlns:xsl="http://www.w3.org/1999/XSL/Transform">
<xsl:output method="html"/>
<!-- content of stylesheet -->
</xsl:stylesheet>
```

Listing 6.22   Specifying HTML as the output format of an XSL stylesheet

The xsl:output must be a child element of the xsl:stylesheet element. It does not have to be the first child, although this is the customary location to place the element.

Once in HTML output mode, the XSLT processor will avoid inserting tags that are not necessary for HTML (such as a closing </br> tag) and will not insert an XML declaration (discussed in the "XML" topic) at the top of the outputted document.

Processing XML

Transforming an XML document through XSLT involves two basic steps. First, you define a mapping from an input XML element and its data to an output format. This first step is accomplished via *templates*. The second step identifies which XML elements to use with each template. This step is known as *matching*. Each step is discussed in the following topics.

Templates

A template is defined within <xsl:template match="..."> tags. The match attribute defines the XML elements that will be processed by this template. For example, to create a template for formatting team elements, you would use the following tag:

```
<xsl:template match="team">
```

Listing 6.23   An xsl:template start tag for matching team elements

Between the opening and closing `xsl:template` tags, you define the output format for the matched element. For example, to create a template that outputs a simple message for every team element in an XML document, you would use the following template:

```
<xsl:template match="team">
  Found a team
</xsl:template>
```

Listing 6.24   A simple template matching team *elements*

This transform would display the same message, "Found a team," once for every team element in the XML document. Note that you can also access and display child element and attribute data from inside the matching element. The transform would be much more effective if we actually displayed information about the team, such as the team name. In a few more sections, we will do precisely this.

Retrieving Information from an Element

You can use the `<xsl:value-of>` element to extract character data, attribute information, or child element information from a matched element. The `select` attribute within the `xsl:value-of` identifies the actual information source (you might take a quick look at Listing 6.26 to get a feel for the syntax). The three most common places from which to retrieve text are the text between the starting and ending element tags of the matched tag (`select="."`), the value of an attribute (`select="@attributeName"`), and the text between the starting and ending tags of a child element (`select="childElementName"`). Note, when retrieving the text between tags (using `select="."` or `select="childElementName"`), all text between the tags, including the text of nested elements, will be included in the result. For example, in Listing 6.25, the text value of the star element is "Vince Carter."

Consider the following XML fragment:

```
<team name="Toronto Raptors">
  <star>Vince Carter</star>
  <coach>Lenny Wilkens</coach>
</team>
```

Listing 6.25   XML fragment describing a team (team.xml)

We can use the following XSLT document to create a simple table from
the team.xml file:

```
<?xml version="1.0"?>
<xsl:stylesheet version="1.0"
    xmlns:xsl="http://www.w3.org/1999/XSL/Transform">
  <xsl:output method="html"/>

  <xsl:template match="team">
    <table border="1">
      <tr>
        <th colspan="2"><xsl:value-of select="@name"/></th>
      </tr>
      <tr>
        <td>COACH</td><td><xsl:value-of select="coach"/></td>
      </tr>
      <tr>
        <td>STAR</td><td><xsl:value-of select="star"/></td>
      </tr>
    </table>
  </xsl:template>
</xsl:stylesheet>
```

Listing 6.26   A simple template

Notice that we can extract multiple pieces of information in a single
template. This XSLT extracts name attribute "Toronto Raptors," and the
values from both the coach and star child tags. Once we process the
XML, the output will be a table similar to Figure 6.1.

Toronto Raptors	
COACH	Lenny Wilkens
STAR	Vince Carter

Figure 6.1   A table containing the contents of Listing 6.25

The actual HTML produced by applying Listing 6.26 to the XML from
Listing 6.25 is:

```
<table border="1">
  <tr>
```

```
   <th colspan="2">Toronto Raptors</th>
 </tr>
 <tr>
    <td>COACH</td>
    <td>Lenny Wilkens</td>
 </tr>
 <tr>
    <td>STAR</td>
    <td>Vince Carter</td>
 </tr>
</table>
```

Listing 6.27   HTML output

Actually, this output has been cleaned up by adding line breaks and indentation. Most XSLT processors will not generate visually pleasing, indented HTML.

Before we move on to discuss template matching in greater detail, you might give some thought to how CSS (Chapter 5) might be incorporated in the XSL of Listing 6.26 to apply complementary colors (Chapter 3) and other styles to make the table more aesthetically appealing. In Chapter 7 we will bring all these elements together to produce an aesthetically pleasing, interactive table.

Matching

In many cases, you can simply use a basic template for each element type in your document. However, stylesheets, by default, begin with the root element of the XML file and look for an element for which there is an associated template in the XSL. Once a template has been found, only that template will be processed. Child elements of the node will not automatically be processed by their templates, even if present. In other words, there is no automatic kick-off where the matched template of a parent element will, once complete, trigger templates for its children; this must be done explicitly by using the xsl:apply-templates element. You may optionally specify which child elements should be processed with the select attribute. If you do not include this attribute, all child elements will be processed. For example, the template in Listing 6.26 can be rewritten as:

```
<xsl:template match="team">
  <table border="1">
    <tr><th colspan="2"><xsl:value-of select="."/>
    <xsl:value-of select="@name"/></th></tr>
```

```
<xsl:apply-templates select="coach"/>
<xsl:apply-templates select="star"/>
</table>
</xsl:template>

<xsl:template match="coach">
<tr><td>COACH</td><td><xsl:value-of select="."/></td></tr>
</xsl:template>

<xsl:template match="star">
<tr><td>STAR</td><td><xsl:value-of select="."/></td></tr>
</xsl:template>
```

Listing 6.28   Matching templates

In the team template, we added two <xsl:apply-template> elements
that tell the XSLT processor to apply any additional templates to
<coach> and <star> elements once the <team> element's template is
complete. In other words, every time a <coach> is encountered in a
<team>, the processor looks for additional templates to apply to <coach>
within the overall <team> template. Listing 6.28 actually generates the
same output as Listing 6.26. In the next topic, "XSLT Flow Control," we
will learn how to add more functionality to the xsl:apply-templates
method by selectively processing elements that match a specified pattern.

Processing from the Root Element

By combining templates and matching, you can define a stylesheet that
will begin transformation from the root element and continue through
every nested element. In order to begin processing from the root element, you must include an xsl:template element with the attribute
match="/". As all elements within an XML document are children of the
root element, you will have to explicitly reference all child elements to
be transformed using xsl:apply-templates elements. Otherwise, the
child elements of an element being handled by a template will be ignored by the XSLT processor. The code of Listing 6.29 demonstrates
how to apply templates beginning at the root element.

```
<?xml version="1.0"?>
<xsl:stylesheet version="1.0"
    xmlns:xsl="http://www.w3.org/1999/XSL/Transform">
<xsl:output method="html"/>
```

```
<xsl:template match="/">
  <!-- no other elements within the document will be transformed
  unless specified by xsl:apply-templates elements. Here we will
  transform all child elements -->
  <xsl:apply-templates/>
</xsl:template>

<!-- templates for child elements
<xsl:template match="childElementType1">
  <!-- processes one type of child element -->
</xsl:template>
<xsl:template match="childElementType2">
  <!-- processes another child element type -->
</xsl:template>

</xsl:stylesheet>
```

Listing 6.29   A stylesheet that will perform transformations starting from the root element

EXAMPLE

For this example, we will transform a simple XML document containing one of William Shakespeare's sonnets (Listing 6.30) into the HTML page shown in Figure 6.2.

```
<?xml version="1.0"?>
<sonnet>
  <title>Sonnet 116</title>
  <author>William Shakespeare</author>
  <line>Let me not to the marriage of true minds</line>
  <line>Admit impediments. Love is not love</line>
  <line>Which alters when it alteration finds,</line>
  <line>Or bends with the remover to remove.</line>
  <line>O no, it is an ever-fixed mark</line>
  <line>That looks on tempests and is never shaken;</line>
  <line>It is the star to every wand'ring bark,</line>
  <line>Whose worth's unknown, although his height be
    taken.</line>
  <line>Love's not time's fool, though rosy lips and
    cheeks</line>
  <line>Within his bending sickle's compass come.</line>
```

```
<line>Love alters not with his brief hours and weeks,</line>
<line>But bears it out ev'n to the edge of doom.</line>
<line>If this be error and upon me proved,</line>
<line>I never writ, nor no man ever loved.</line>
</sonnet>
```

Listing 6.30   sonnet116.xml

This XML, when transformed, will result in the nicely formatted sonnet in Figure 6.2.

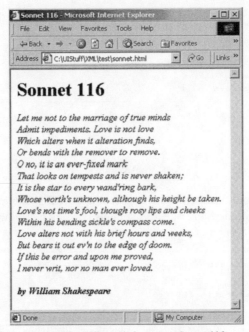

Figure 6.2   William Shakespeare's Sonnet 116

By examining the desired result (Figure 6.2), we can see that each line element in sonnet116.xml needs to be italicized. We will also display the author's name in bold italics and use a header (h1) element to display the title. The stylesheet that will perform this translation is shown in Listing 6.31. Notice that we use xsl:apply-templates so that the XSLT processor will process not only the <sonnet> element, but all elements nested within the <sonnet> element.

```
<?xml version="1.0"?>
<xsl:stylesheet version="1.0"
```

```
    xmlns:xsl="http://www.w3.org/1999/XSL/Transform">
<xsl:output method="html"/>


<!-- opens the HTML comments and applies the templates for other
    elements -->
<xsl:template match="sonnet">
  <html>
    <head><title><xsl:value-of select="title"/></title></head>
    <xsl:apply-templates select="title"/>
    <xsl:apply-templates select="line"/>
    <xsl:apply-templates select="author"/>
  </html>
</xsl:template>


<!-- places the title in h1 headings -->
<xsl:template match="title">
  <h1><xsl:value-of select="."/></h1>
</xsl:template>


<!-- italicizes each line and places a newline tag at the end of
    each line -->
<xsl:template match="line">
  <i><xsl:value-of select="."/></i><br/>
</xsl:template>


<!-- bolds and italicizes the author -->
<xsl:template match="author">
  <p><b><i>by <xsl:value-of select="."/></i></b></p>
</xsl:template>
</xsl:stylesheet>
```

Listing 6.31   transformSonnet.xsl

HOW AND WHY

How Can I Format My XML According to a Stylesheet on the Browser?
Rather than running the XSLT processor on the command line, you can
add a directive instructing the client's browser to perform the transform.
Simply include the following line at the start of your XML file (after the
XML declaration).

```
<?xml-stylesheet type="text/xsl" href="urlOfStylesheet"?>
```

Listing 6.32   The XSL stylesheet processing instruction

For example, if you wish to format an XML document according to the stylesheet located at www.codenotes.com/stylesheets/mysheet.xsl, your XML document would look similar to the following:

```
<?xml version="1.0"?>
<?xml-stylesheet type="text/xml"
    href="www.codenotes.com/stylesheets/mysheet.xsl"?>
<root>
  <!-- rest of document -->
</root>
```

Listing 6.33   A sample XML document that will be transformed by the web browser

Any XML-enabled browser will automatically perform the transformation for you. However, at this time, the only fully XML- and XSL-enabled browsers are IE 5.0 and higher. For now, XML and XSLT are more often applied on the server through ASP, PHP, Perl, Servlet, or JSP systems.

SUMMARY

Using XSLT, you can create templates for each XML element that will be fired when the XML element is encountered by the XSLT processor. The templates can transform the XML into HTML output. Using simple matching criteria, you can extract information from a particular tag, its attributes, and its children. In order to build an XSLT transform, you should follow these steps:

1. Add the document definition `<?xml version="1.0"?>`.
2. Set the output method using `<xsl:output method="HTML">`.
3. Add templates for each element using `<xsl:template match="your element name">` tags. Remember that you can use `<xsl:apply-templates select="childnode">` to apply additional templates to child elements.
4. Within a template, use `<xsl:value-of select="whatever">` to select content from the element matched by the template. The value of the select statement can be "." (the current node content), "@attribute name" for the value of an attribute, or the name of a child node.

In the next topic, you will see several enhancements to basic template matching that allow you to iteratively process elements using loops and complex searches.

Topic: XSLT Flow Control

This topic presents methods for using XSLT to mimic basic control flow statements such as loops and if..else statements. In addition, this topic explores XPath, which is a simple query language that greatly expands the power of the select attributes used in <xsl:template>, <xsl:apply-templates>, and <xsl:value-of> tags.

CONCEPTS

XPath Introduction
XPath is a simple query language that is used within the select or match attributes of XSL elements. For example, by using an XPath statement for the select attribute of an xsl:apply-templates element, you specify that a template should fire only if a <person> element has a firstName attribute of "Mike." A select attribute so constructed will no longer be globally applied to all <person> elements.

```
<xsl:apply-templates
    select="person/[@firstName='Mike']@firstName"/>
```

Listing 6.34   Templates to be applied only if a person has a firstName *attribute of "Mike"*

The actual code used in this listing will make more sense after working through a few additional concepts.

XPath treats an XML document as a tree, where the root node of the document is the trunk and each child element is a branch. Additional grandchild elements are branches off of child branches, and so on. In one sense, element attributes are leaves, as an attribute cannot have any child elements.

Earlier in this topic, we encountered some simple XPath statements. In fact, any value that we have used for the select attribute of an xol:value-of clomont or xsl:apply-templates element and the match attribute of an xsl:template element is an XPath statement (for example, the ".", "@attributeName," and "childName" operators discussed in "Retrieving Information from an Element" are all basic XPath statements).

Basic Tree Traversal

If you are familiar with directory traversal on Unix machines, you will recognize the syntax for basic tree traversal in XPath (if you are a Windows user, the only difference is that a "/" is used instead of "\"). Generally, paths lead to a particular element. If you need to access an attribute within an element, you must preface the attribute name with the @ symbol.

As with directory traversal, there are two basic types of XPath statements: absolute and relative. Absolute statements begin traversal from the root element of the XML document, whereas relative statements begin from the current element.

All absolute statements start with "/" and continuously specify child elements (or attributes) separated by a "/". For example, to specify <arena> element (bold) in the following XML document:

```
<?xml version="1.0"?>
<hockey>
  <team name="Boston Bruins">
    <arena>Fleet Center</arena>
  </team>
</hockey>
```

Listing 6.35   A sample XML document for storing details about a hockey team

you could use the select attribute of the following xsl:value-of element:

```
<xsl:value-of select="/hockey/team/arena"/>
```

Listing 6.36   A simple absolute XPath statement

As an alternative to repeatedly using absolute statements, you can also use relative statements to specify a location. Relative statements start from the most recently accessed element. For example, the following XSLT template will also match the boldfaced element in Listing 6.35:

```
<xsl:template match="hockey">
  <h2>Arena - <xsl:value-of select="team/arena"/></h2>
</xsl:template>
```

Listing 6.37   A simple relative XPath statement

Because the <xsl:template> tag selects a <hockey> element, the <xsl:value-of> element can use a relative path to select the arena child of the team element using a relative path.

The Parent-of Element

As with traversing a directory, it is also possible to use XPath to retrace steps (traverse to the parent element). You can work backward through the tree by using the parent-of operator (..). The template in Listing 6.38 uses the parent-of operator to display the name of a team as well as the arena it plays in (using the XML document from Listing 6.35).

```
<xsl:template match="arena">
  <xsl:value-of select="."/>
    is the home arena of the
    <xsl:value-of select="../@name"/>
</xsl:template>
```

Listing 6.38   Using the parent-of operator

The resulting output for XSL of Listing 6.38 is shown in Listing 6.39. Here we use .. to retrieve the arena element's parent element (team) and then, using the @ prefix, we retrieve the value of the name attribute. The select="." attribute (mentioned in the "Templates" concept) is used to retrieve the text within the current arena element.

```
Fleet Center is the home arena of the Boston Bruins
```

Listing 6.39   Output of Listing 6.38

The Wildcard Element

You will often wish to match all elements at a specific traversal level. For example, imagine you are transforming an XML list of club members similar to Listing 6.40.

```
<club>
  <president><name>Mike Van Atter</name></president>
  <vicePres><name>Dan Jay</name></vicePres>
  <eventMgr><name>Matt Jay</name></eventMgr>
  <!-- continues ... -->
</club>
```

Listing 6.40   An XML format for storing club members names

In this XML file, the name element occurs in many different tags, but always at the same nested level. If you simply wanted to print out each employee's name in an identical fashion, you could use the wildcard character "*" to match all elements at a specific level. The select attribute of the xsl:apply-templates element shown in Listing 6.41 uses this wildcard to match all child elements of the club element so that each name element can be retrieved no matter what its parent element happens to be.

```
<xsl:apply-templates select="/club/*/name"/>
```

*Listing 6.41   Using * to match all elements at a single nested level*

A Global Search

Another useful feature when traversing XML documents using XPath is the global search operator (//). The // operator can be used to find all elements or attributes of a specific type, regardless of their location in the document. Depending on whether a "." is present before the // operator, // will search either all elements in the entire XML document or all elements nested within the current element as shown in Table 6.2.

Search	Output
`<xsl:apply-templates select="//stock"/>`	Will apply templates on all stock elements in the entire XML document
`<xsl:apply-templates select=".//stock"/>`	Will apply templates on all stock elements that are descendants of the current element.

Table 6.2   Using the // operator

Filters

Filters allow you to further refine your XPath statements using boolean expressions that evaluate to either true or false. Elements for which the boolean expression evaluates to true are included in the final XPath statement. Filter expressions are separated from the rest of the XPath statement by square brackets [ ].

The following xsl:value-of element will display the value of a goals attribute only if it is greater than zero.

```
<xsl:value-of select="current()[@goals > 0]/@goals"/>
```

Listing 6.42   A simple filter for displaying the value of goal attributes

The [@goals > 0] component tells the processor to use only elements at the current level with an attribute of goals that has a value greater than 0. This expression does not change the location in the tree, so you have to specify the element again after the filter to display the value of the goals attribute. You will notice that in Listing 6.42 we used the `current()` operator before the filter. The `current()` function is used with filters when you wish to perform filters on the current element. You can use the `current()` function at anytime; it simply performs the same as a ".".

Boolean Conditions

In addition to the greater-than operator (>), you can use any of the operators in Table 6.3. Notice that `&lt;` is used instead of "<" so that your XPath statements will conform to XML syntax (where "<" indicates the beginning of a new element).

Symbol	Meaning	Symbol	Meaning
=	equal	>	greater than
!=	not equal	>=	greater than or equal to
&lt;	less than	and	logical and
<=	less than or equal to	or	logical or
not	logical not	()	grouping

Table 6.3   XPath boolean operators

Each of these conditions is case-sensitive, and you can combine conditions within a filter using parentheses. For example [(@count>10) and (@name='Wayne')] filters for elements with a count attribute greater than 10 and a name attribute equal to Wayne.

Filters can appear multiple times within your XPath as well as appearing in any part of your XPath statement. Consider the XML in Listing 6.43.

```
<HallOfFame>
  <player firstName="Wayne" lastName="Gretzky">
    <bestSeason>
      <year>85-86</year>
      <stats goals="52" assists="163"/>
    </bestSeason>
  </player>
  <player firstName="Mario" lastName="Lemieux">
    <bestSeason>
      <year>00-09</year>
      <stats goals="85" assists="114"/>
    </bestSeason>
```

```
</player>
</HallOfFame>
```

Listing 6.43   A searchable XML document

You can use XPath filters to find very specific components in this file. For example, you could extract Wayne's best season, the years that anyone scored over 60 goals, or the last name of any player named Mario:

```
<!-- note: the following statements are simply sections of an
     XSLT document and do not represent an entire file -->

<!-- Statement 1 Wayne's best year will print 85-86 -->
<xsl:value-of
select="/HallOfFame/player[@firstName='Wayne']/bestSeason/year"
/>

<!-- Statement 2 Any year where someone scored over 60 goals,
will only print 88-89 -->
<xsl:template match="bestSeason">
  <xsl:value-of select="stats[@goals > 60]/../year"/>
</xsl:template>

<!-- Statement 3 Last name of players named Mario, prints
Lemieux -->
<xsl:template match="player">
  <xsl:value-of select="current()[@firstName='Mario']/@lastName"
/>
</xsl:template>
```

Listing 6.44   XPath filter examples

Statement 1 is an absolute path, starting from the root of the XML document, that uses a filter in the middle of the path to select specific players by first name. Notice that because the XPath statement is within an attribute, we had to use different quotes to delimit the string literal "Wayne."

Statement 2 is an example of using a relative XPath statement. In this statement, we are starting at a bestSeason element thanks to the <xsl:template> tag. The filter is used to ensure that only seasons with more than 60 goals will be displayed. We also used the parent-of-operator (..) so that we could retrace our steps to find the value of the associated year element.

Statement 3 is another relative XPath statement. Here we use the filter on the current element, so we must start our XPath statement with the current() function.

Control Flow within XSLT

In addition to providing an element query language (XPath), XSLT also allows you to perform some simple control flow statements. In particular, this concept illustrates using XPath to loop through elements, sort elements, and perform conditional operations (if statements).

Looping

The xsl:for-each element allows you to loop through all elements matching criteria specified by an XPath statement. Each xsl:for-each element has a select attribute that uses an XPath statement to define the elements to be processed. As with xsl:template elements, the text between the <xsl:for-each> and </xsl:for-each> tags details the formatting for the specified elements. The xsl:for-each element is basically an alternative to using xsl:apply-templates to call an xsl:templates element, as illustrated in Listing 6.45.

```
<!-- prints out the text of each child element -->
<xsl:for-each select="*">
  <h1><xsl:value-of select="."/></h1>
</xsl:for-each>
```

Listing 6.45   Using xsl:for-each to print the contents of each child element

In Listing 6.45, we use the * wildcard (discussed in the "Basic Tree Traversal" concept) to match all child elements of the current element. Within this loop, we simply display the value of each child element as an HTML heading. The <xsl:for-each> element in combination with the * wildcard, saves us the trouble of having to create a separate call to <xsl:apply-templates> for every type of child element that might be encountered inside the current element.

Sorting

When you process multiple elements in one step (as is the case with xsl:for-each and xsl:apply-template elements), you can sort the elements before the elements are processed. This sorting is done using the xsl:sort element with three attributes: select, order, and data-type. The select attribute defines the element or attribute to use as the sorting key. The order attribute can be either "ascending" or "descending," and describes the order of the sort. Finally, the data-type can be either "number" or "text," telling the XSL processor to sort numerically or alphabetically. The xsl:sort element must appear as a nested element of the corresponding selection element (either <xsl:for-each> or <xsl:apply-templates>).

For example, to sort all player elements by their name attribute before applying the appropriate template, you would use the following code:

```
<xsl:apply-templates select="player">
  <xsl:sort select="@name" order="ascending" data-type="text"/>
</xsl:apply-templates>
```

Listing 6.46   Sorting all player elements by the name attribute

Be aware that the alphabetical sorting order may be different for different parsers. The SAXON parser, for instance, uses a case-insensitive sort generating [Apple, apple, Bear, bear], whereas Microsoft's MSMXL parser generates [apple, Apple, bear, Bear]. In other words, do not assume that the <xsl:sort> element will return the same order for all systems.

If and Choose

In addition to XPath, XSL provides two other means for performing conditional operations. The xsl:if element is used in a manner similar to that of an if statement in a normal programming language. The condition for the if statement is contained in a test attribute. However, unlike most standard if statements, there is no accompanying xsl:else-if or xsl:else element. The following simple example displays a simple message if a person has been promoted:

```
<xsl:if test="@promotion='yes'">
  Received a promotion
</xsl:if>
```

Listing 6.47   Using xsl:if

If you want to mimic an if-else structure, you will need to use the xsl:choose element. This structure is very similar to a switch or case statement, as the following code sample demonstrates:

```
<xsl:choose>
  <xsl:when test="@sex='male'">You are a guy</xsl:when>
  <xsl:when test="@sex='female'">You are a girl</xsl:when>
  <xsl:otherwise>What are you?</xsl:otherwise>
</xsl:choose>
```

Listing 6.48   A simple xsl:choose element

Each xsl:choose element must have at least one xsl:when element; however, the presence of an xsl:otherwise element is entirely optional. It is important to note that the first matching xsl:when element will be used, even if other conditions also evaluate to true. The output associated with the xsl:otherwise element will be displayed only if all of the xsl:when test attributes evaluate to false.

EXAMPLE

In this example, we will transform a simple XML document listing contact information into an HTML table. For the purposes of identifying those closest to us, we will bold the phone number of people who live in New York, italicize the addresses of those who live in the United States, and leave the rest of the information in base font. To make it easier to find the contact information for a specific individual, we will sort the entries in the final table by last name. We will take the XML of Listing 6.49 and, by transforming it through the XSL of Listing 6.50, we will end up with the HTML table shown in Figure 6.3.

```
<?xml version="1.0"?>
<contacts>
  <contact>
    <name first="Paul" last="Robertson"/>
    <country>England</country>
    <phoneNum>01293 555 432</phoneNum>
  </contact>
  <contact>
    <name first="Tamsin" last="Anderson"/>
    <country>Canada</country>
    <phoneNum>519 234 7890</phoneNum>
  </contact>
  <contact>
    <name first="Kevin" last="O'Flaherty"/>
    <country state="NY">United States</country>
    <phoneNum>212 987 3214</phoneNum>
  </contact>
  <contact>
    <name first="Mike" last="Robinson"/>
    <country state="Mass">United States</country>
    <phoneNum>339 675 3245</phoneNum>
```

```
  </contact>
</contacts>
```

Listing 6.49   contacts.xml

My phone numbers		
FIRST	LAST	NUMBER
Tamsin	Anderson	519 234 7890
Kevin	O'Flaherty	**212 987 3214**
Paul	Robertson	01293 555 432
Mike	Robinson	*339 675 3245*

Figure 6.3   Displaying contact information

The stylesheet to perform this transformation is shown in Listing 6.50.

```
<?xml version="1.0"?>
<xsl:stylesheet version="1.0"
    xmlns:xsl="http://www.w3.org/1999/XSL/Transform">
<xsl:output method="html"/>

<!-- template for root element sets up the table -->
<xsl:template match="/">
  <html>
  <head><title>My Contacts</title></head>
  <body>
   <table border="1">
     <tr><th colspan="3">My phone numbers</th></tr>
     <tr><td>FIRST</td><td>LAST</td><td>NUMBER</td></tr>

     <!-- apply phoneNum template after sorting by last name -->
     <xsl:apply-templates select="contacts/contact/phoneNum">
       <xsl:sort select="../name/@last" order="ascending"
          data-type="text"/>
     </xsl:apply-templates>
     </table>
  </body>
  </html>
</xsl:template>
```

```
<!-- template for each phone number -->
<xsl:template match="phoneNum">
<tr><td><xsl:value-of select="../name/@last"/></td>
  <td><xsl:value-of select="../name/@first"/></td>
  <td>
    <!-- format text according to country and state -->
    <xsl:choose>
      <xsl:when test="../country='United States' and
        ../country/@state='NY'">
        <b><xsl:value-of select="."/></b>
      </xsl:when>
      <xsl:when test="../country='United States'">
        <i><xsl:value-of select="."/></i>
      </xsl:when>
      <xsl:otherwise><xsl:value-of select="."/></xsl:otherwise>
    </xsl:choose>
  </td>
</tr>
</xsl:template>
</xsl:stylesheet>
```

Listing 6.50   transformNums.xsl

For the most part, transformNums.xsl consists of HTML code for creating the table (the `<table>`, `<tr>`, and `<td>` elements) and a little bit of XSL. The first set of boldfaced lines (shown again in Listing 6.51) uses the xsl:sort element to sort all elements before applying the template. Also, notice how the *parent-of* operator (..) is used to traverse upward to the parent element of phoneNum (contact) in order to retrieve the corresponding phone number.

```
<xsl:apply-templates select="contacts/contact/phoneNum">
  <xsl:sort select="../name/@last" order="ascending"
    data-type="text"/>
</xsl:apply-templates>
```

Listing 6.51   Sorting and applying the templates

The second section of boldfaced code (shown again in Listing 6.52) provides different formatting for each phone number. We used a simple xsl:choose element to mimic an if..else structure. Notice that the first xsl:when tests if the contact is in the United States and in New York, while the second xsl:when tests only if the person is located in the United States.

```
<xsl:choose>
  <xsl:when test="../country='United States' and
    ../country/@state='NY'">
    <b><xsl:value-of select="."/></b>
  </xsl:when>
  <xsl:when test="../country='United States'">
    <i><xsl:value-of select="."/></i>
  </xsl:when>
  <xsl:otherwise><xsl:value-of select="."/></xsl:otherwise>
</xsl:choose>
```

Listing 6.52   Formatting the phone number according to location

The final output of Listing 6.50 when used on the data in Listing 6.49 is shown in Listing 6.53.

```
<html>
    <head>
        <title>My Contacts</title>
    </head>
    <body>
        <table border="1">
            <tr>
                <th colspan="3">My phone numbers</th>
            </tr>
            <tr>
                <td>LAST</td>
                <td>FIRST</td>
                <td>NUMBER</td>
            </tr>
            <tr>
                <td>Tamsin</td>
                <td>Anderson</td>
                <td>519 234 789</td>
            </tr>
            <tr>
                <td>Kevin</td>
                <td>O'Flaherty</td>
                <td><b>212 987 321</b></td>
            </tr>
            <tr>
```

```
        <td>Paul</td>
        <td>Robertson</td>
        <td>01293 555 432</td>
      </tr>
      <tr>
        <td>Mike</td>
        <td>Robinson</td>
        <td><i>339 675 324</i></td>
      </tr>
    </table>
  </body>
</html>
```

Listing 6.53   phoneNums.html

HOW AND WHY

Can I Sort on Multiple Keys?

Yes, it is possible to sort on multiple keys. List the keys, starting with the most important key, in multiple xsl:sort elements. For example, if we wanted to sort by last name and then first name in Listing 6.50, you would use the following code:

```
<xsl:apply-templates select="contacts/contact/phoneNum">
  <xsl:sort select="../name/@last" order="ascending"
      data-type="text"/>
  <xsl:sort select="../name/@first" order="ascending"
      data-type="text"/>
</xsl:apply-templates>
```

Listing 6.54   Sorting by multiple keys

DESIGN NOTES

Global Searches

The global search operator (//) exhaustively searches each element within your XML document. For large XML files, this can be very time-consuming. You should limit your use of the global search operator to situations when you know you will be dealing with small documents or occasions where you have no other alternative.

SUMMARY

XPath adds tremendous flexibility to the basic XSLT transformation. Any place that an XSLT element has a `select` or `match` attribute, you use an XPath statement to perform a search with optional filtering. The syntax for XPath follows a simple tree structure, where each branch is divided by a "/" character, and attributes are identified with the "@" character. An XPath statement can be absolute (from the root node) or relative to the currently selected node.

With regard to flow control, XSLT uses `<xsl:apply-templates>` and `<xsl:for-each>` elements to process a collection of child elements. The element collection may be sorted by adding an `<xsl:sort>` tag as a child element to either of the collection tags. The sort may be numeric or text based, in ascending or descending order, and may match on any attribute or child element.

Finally, the `<xsl:if>` and `<xsl:choose>` elements provide a simple logical branching system for your XSLT documents. You can use these elements to conditionally apply a transformation based on attribute values or element text.

Topic: Using XML and XSLT to Support All Browser Versions

After reading this chapter, it may become apparent that XML and XSLT can be leveraged to solve the common problem of supporting the many different browser versions and vendors. Specifically, if we separate our web content into XML files, and place our DHTML presentation and logic in XSLT files (different XSLT transformations for different browsers), we can avoid:

- "Dumbing down" the HTML and DHTML to the lowest common browser denominator and not taking advantage of any dynamic capabilities. We can use a different XSLT to generate HTML and DHTML for the particular browser type.
- Writing multiple versions of our website for different browsers. Rather than rewriting the entire site, we can simply change small sections of our XSLT.
- Writing forking, redundant JavaScript (i.e., determining browser type on the client and running different code sections depending on version).

This topic illustrates a typical conversion process for moving from HTML and JavaScript to XML/XSLT.

CONCEPTS

Simple Example
This simple example demonstrates how to convert raw HTML/DHTML into an XML/XSLT structure. To begin, examine Listing 6.55, which generates a typical DHTML effect.

```
<HTML>
<script language=javascript>
  function highlight(e, b)
  {
    var src;
    // Fork for Netscape event handling
    if (navigator.appName == "Netscape")
      src =  e.target;
    else
      src = e.srcElement;
     if(b)
     {
       src.origColor=src.style.backgroundColor;
       src.style.backgroundColor="darkkhaki";
     }
     else
     {
       src.style.backgroundColor=src.origColor;
     }
  }
</script>
<BODY>
  <p onmouseover="highlight(event,true)"
     onmouseout="highlight(event,false)">
     Highlight me on mouseover! </p>
</BODY>
</HTML>
```

Listing 6.55 A simple DHTML highlight effect

When rendered by a browser, the DHTML of Listing 6.55 will produce a single line of text reading "Highlight me on mouseover!" When the mouse is positioned over the text, its background will change to a dark khaki, and when the mouse leaves the text, it will revert to the standard browser background.

While this DHTML works correctly, it is nonoptimal for a few reasons:

1. The simple effect requires a significant amount of boilerplate code.
2. Additional, redundant code needs to be included (boldfaced text) to accommodate different browsers.
3. Data, presentation, and logic are completely and inseparably intermixed.

We can address all three of these negative points by using XML and XSLT to separate our data and presentation.

Moving to XML/XSLT
Our data for this example is quite simple; in XML it would appear as:

```
<note> Highlight me on mouseover! </note>
```

Listing 6.56   Data separated into XML

Note that our XML element name of "note" is purely arbitrary; we could call the element anything you like. It is, of course, better to be precise with tag names so that those reading your XML can figure out what is likely to happen when it is run through an XSLT transform such as that shown in Listing 6.57.

```
<?xml version="1.0"?>
<xsl:stylesheet version="1.0"
    xmlns:xsl="http://www.w3.org/1999/XSL/Transform">
  <xsl:output method="html"/>

<xsl:template match="/">
  <script language="javascript">
  <![CDATA[
    function highlight(e,b)
    {
      var src;
      // Fork for Netscape event handling
      if (document.all)
        src = e.srcElement;
```

```
    else
      src = e.target;
    //switch colors
    if(b)
    {
      src.origColor=src.style.backgroundColor;
      src.style.backgroundColor="darkkhaki";
    }
    else
    {
      src.style.backgroundColor=src.origColor;
    }
  }
]]>
</script>

<xsl:apply-templates select="./note" />
</xsl:template>

<xsl:template match="highlight">
  <p onmouseover="highlight(event,true)"
    onmouseout="highlight(event,false)">
    <xsl:value-of select="text()"/></p>

</xsl:template>
</xsl:stylesheet>
```

Listing 6.57   Generic XSL for a highlight effect

Assuming the XML of Listing 6.56 exists in a file called highlight.xml and is run "through" the XSL transform of Listing 6.57 (highlight.xsl)

```
saxon highlight.xml highlight.xsl
```

you will end up with the HTML of Listing 6.55.

Browser Support

Moving to XML/XSLT doesn't directly solve all of the problems. Recall the code that differentiates between Netscape and IE versions (bold-faced in Listing 6.55). We can modify our XSL to produce the correct HTML for the appropriate browser. If we modify the XML by adding a new attribute (called "browser") so that we have

```
<?xml version="1.0"?>
<highlight browser="Netscape"> Highlight me When clicked!
</highlight>
```

Listing 6.58   Modified XML

we can modify our XSL of Listing 6.57 to produce precisely correct DHTML by reading the browser attribute and acting accordingly. Simply replace the Netscape/IE forking code in our XSL with:

```
//prior code is identical to Listing 6.57
var src;
// Fork for Netscape event handling
   <xsl:choose>
     <xsl:when test="highlight/@browser = 'Netscape'">
       src =e.srcElement</xsl:when>
     <xsl:when test="highlight/@browser = 'IE'">
       src=e.target</xsl:when>
   </xsl:choose>
   //switch colors
   if(b)
//remaining code remains unchanged and is omitted for brevity
```

Listing 6.59   Placing the Netscape/IE fork in XSL

We now have an XSL transform that produces precisely the correct DHTML effect code for the particular browser. Our XML is simple and easy to read, and our XSLT is easily modifiable and suitably generic. With some enhancements, this XSL file can provide highlighting effects whenever and wherever we need them to any type of element. In other words, we can write the code once and use it everywhere.

A Multitarget XSL Transform Architecture

Admittedly, the example in the preceding section is somewhat simplified. However, if we include the browser type as an attribute in the XML document (or determine it on the server by examining the HTML request headers), we can build a web architecture to target any browser we like. The basic steps are to separate all data into XML and create a series of XSL files containing our presentation logic, layout, and effects. We might have one or more XSL files for each browser version we wanted to target, as illustrated in Figure 6.4.

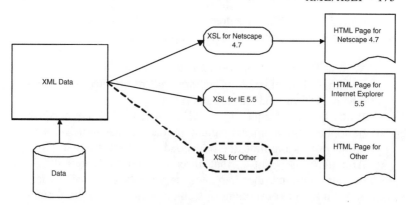

Figure 6.4   If data is in XML, presentation logic can be stored in multiple XSL transforms,
one or more for each target browser

The architecture shown in Figure 6.4 has definite advantages and some drawbacks. Enumerating the advantages first:

1. Complete separation of data and presentation logic allows for a modular architecture. You can accommodate any browser or, for that matter, any kind of output for any device, from handheld computers to web-enabled cell phones.
2. Whenever a new browser or device comes about, you do not have to modify any existing XSL or code. You simply create a new transform. It becomes very difficult to break existing functionality.
3. Such architectures result in cheaper cost of ownership and maintenance for large development groups. Web developers and programmers can work on XSL transforms, where less technical professionals can concentrate on the XML data and not be exposed to (and confused by) DHTML syntax.
4. XSL files may include other XSL files and may even, themselves, be further transformed by XSL files. This gives the architect the ability to isolate and translate DHTML functionality at any granularity.
5. Relational databases are evolving toward this style of architecture. Databases are beginning to incorporate more XML/XSL/ HTML-based tools and features. It is entirely conceivable that, in the near future, the distinction between web servers and relational databases will disappear and a DBMS system, such as Oracle, will "host" its data as HTML pages created by translating XML-formatted relational data through XSL transforms.

However, this architecture does have some drawbacks. Some of the disadvantages of the multitarget XSL approach are as follows:

1. Most web development tools are not designed to accommodate this kind of architecture. They are built to produce web pages where DHTML and data are intertwined.
2. If data changes frequently, the XML-XSLT transform needs to be applied in real time with great frequency. Each translation requires processing time and download time for the new HTML. Although this is not all that different from conventional ASP or JSP solutions, there are not, as yet, standardized, widely adopted server conventions or technologies to cache these kinds of translations.
3. Most current web servers and server-side web technologies do not have built-in capability for translating XML via XSL and returning the resulting HTML. In all likelihood, you would have to design and implement this architecture on the server side, perhaps by authoring special ASP or JSP pages that perform the translation action.
4. Server-side web technologies such as Microsoft's ASP.NET (in beta at the time of this writing) provide similar functionality. ASP.NET provides the ability to create forms and write code on the server side in the drag-and-drop fashion of Visual Basic. What is extraordinary, however, is that ASP.NET will automatically render the appropriate DHTML for the browser that is requesting the page. If you are willing to adopt a proprietary technology such as ASP.NET, it may render the multitarget XSL approach unnecessary.

SUMMARY

In the final analysis, only you can determine whether a multitarget XSL approach is worthwhile. But it may even be that, with time, this is the approach the industry will come to embrace. Unless one company or group is able to emerge as the sole browser vendor, it is exceedingly likely that there will always be irritating differences between the features supported by different browsers as each tries to outdo the other.

Regardless of whether you choose to employ XSL and XML today, understanding the power of XML and XSL is certain to make your web development easier in the future.

Chapter Summary

The Extensible Markup Language (XML) has rapidly become one of the most pervasive and widely adopted formats for storing data. With the added power of the Extensible Stylesheet Language Transformation (XSLT), XML can be transformed into any format, including HTML, using a very simple language. In the near future, you may find that HTML will begin to look more and more like XML, and that XML and XSLT will play an increasingly important role in developing web page content. In fact, the XHTML standard presently recommended by the W3C ⌁UI060001 is an XML-compliant upgrade to regular HTML.

You can use XML and XSLT to separate your data from its presentation, creating a highly adaptable system that can generate content for a wide variety of browsers and consumers. You could, for instance, use one XSLT to transform XML data into color-enhanced HTML, and another XSLT to add browser-specific JavaScript features. With fairly simple changes, you can customize the web experience for a user based on browser type and user options. This flexibility makes it much easier to follow the basic rules of good web user interface design.

For a more thorough discussion of XML and XSLT, see *CodeNotes for XML.*

Chapter 7

—

TABLES

HTML tables were originally intended to do nothing more than display tabular data. However, tables have evolved into a mechanism to control the layout of elements in almost every web page. Tables allow designers to create a layout grid used for text columns, images, and chart-oriented data. Even though CSS offers the ability to position content exactly (see the "CSS Positioning" concept in Chapter 5), tables offer the much needed ability to arrange your page in rows and columns. Without using tables, it is extremely difficult to position elements next to each other.

In this chapter, we are going to look at how to use HTML tables in conjunction with CSS, JavaScript, DHTML, and XML/XSLT to display tabular data, including HTML elements, in a sophisticated, aesthetically pleasing, and interactive manner that will rival the best of traditional nonweb applications.

SIMPLE APPLICATION

The simplest possible table may be created using the uninspired code in Listing 7.1.

```
<table border="1">
    <tr><th>Simple Table</th></tr>
    <tr><td>File</td></tr>
    <tr><td>Edit</td></tr>
```

```
    <tr><td>View</td></tr>
    <tr><td>Project</td></tr>
</table>
```

Listing 7.1   Simple table

The result, in a browser, of Listing 7.1 is:

Figure 7.1   A noninteractive HTML table

| **Simple Table** |
| File |
| Edit |
| View |
| Project |

The table contains one table header <th>, and four table rows, each consisting of one <td>, or table-data element. Clearly, this table is neither
interactive nor visually appealing. In the course of this chapter, we will
provide a thorough makeover for this simple example.

Topic: Basic Tables

CONCEPTS

Basic Table Elements
The basic table element, <table>, defines the beginning of the table, and
it is usually followed by the optional table header <th>, and then one or
many table records <tr>, each one of which may contain one or many
data elements, or columns <td>.

Note that the <th> is optional and does nothing more than make the
header information bold. There is also an optional <caption> element
(not shown) that will place a label above, below, to the left, or to the
right of the table via the align attribute (<caption align="top">). Addi-
tionally, there are 8 to 10 (depending on your browser) borderstyle at-
tributes, allowing you to select different graphical border types. (See
⟳UI070001 for a table of these and other values.)

The basic elements of a table are child elements:

- `<caption>` Table caption will produce a caption above, below, to the right, or to the left of the table via its align attribute.
- `<tr>` Table row contains one or many `<td>` elements (or columns).
- `<th>` Table header puts data in the top row in bold. Use `<th>` to replace the `<tr>` tag for the first row of data.
- `<td>` Table data. Each `<td>` element must be contained within a `<tr>` or `<th>` element, and represents one column of data.

Additional lesser-used elements (introduced in HTML 4.0):

- `<thead>` Defines a table header section.
- `<tbody>` Defines a table body.
- `<tfoot>` Defines a table-footnote section.

The purpose of these divisions is to allow scrolling through the body of a large table while both the header and footer sections remain in place, as well as formatting each table section for style purposes.

Column-Based Tables
Most tables are defined as rows, then columns. It is possible, however, to design the table using column-based notation. The two relevant tags are:

- `<col>` Used to assign attribute values to individual columns within a colgroup.
- `<colgroup>` Defines a group of columns in a table (see col).

In Listing 7.2, you can see how to use these tags to create a different width for each column in a table. This table will appear similar to the one shown in Figure 7.2. As discussed in "CSS Positioning" in Chapter 5, relative positioning (using percentages) ensures the page can be viewed on various sizes of browser window.

```
<HTML>
<table>
<colgroup>
<col width="20%">
<col width="30%">
<col width="15%">
</colgroup>
<tr>
<th>First Column Header</th>
<th>Second Column Header</th>
```

```
<th>Third Column Header</th>
</tr>
<tr><td>cell 1,2</td><td>cell 2,2</td><td>cell 3,2</td></tr>
<tr><td>cell 1,3</td><td>cell 2,3</td><td>cell 3,3</td></tr>
</table>
</HTML>
```

Listing 7.2   Creating a column group

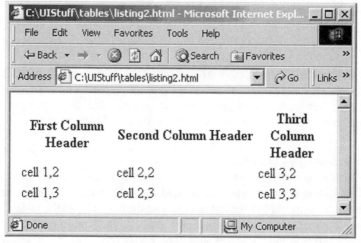

Figure 7.2   Output of Listing 7.2

Spanning

By default, table rows are homogeneous. That is, each row contains the same number of columns. Similarly, each column spans the same number of rows. You can control this feature using column and row spanning. For example, consider the table in Figure 7.3.

Simple Table	Blank
File	Open
Edit	
View	
Project	

Figure 7.3   Column and row spanning

This table can be generated by applying the `colspan` or `rowspan` attributes to <td> elements, as illustrated in Listing 7.3.

```
<table border="1">
  <tr><th>Simple Table</th><th>Blank</th></tr>
  <tr><td>File</td><td rowspan=2>Open</td></tr>
  <tr><td>Edit</td></tr>
  <tr><td colspan=2>View</td></td></tr>
  <tr><td colspan=2>Project</td></tr>
</table>
```

Listing 7.3   Utilizing colspan and rowspan

Notice that the attribute is always applied to a <td> element. The `rowspan` attribute forces the cell to span two or more rows, as illustrated by the Open cell. The `colspan` attribute forces the cell to span two or more columns, as illustrated by both the View and Project cells.

Table Borders and Padding

In all the examples so far, we have used the table attribute `border="1"`. By including this attribute, you are telling the browser to include a visible border surrounding the entire table and the cells within the table. The value of the attribute (a small integer) indicates the size, in pixels, of the border surrounding the entire table. The size of the border (in pixels) between each cell is controlled by the table's `cellspacing` attribute. If you wish to adjust the padding between a cell's contents and the border, you can adjust the `cellpadding` attribute. The difference between these attributes is best demonstrated through examples. In Listing 7.4, we create a cell with a small `cellspacing` attribute (creating a small border between cells) and a large `cellpadding` attribute (creating a large space between borders and cells). The output of Listing 7.4 is shown in Figure 7.4. In Listing 7.5 and Figure 7.5 we create a table with the opposite characteristics: a large `cellspacing` attribute and a small `cellpadding` attribute.

```
<table border="4" cellspacing="1" cellpadding="5">
  <tr><td>cell 1</td><td>cell 2</td></tr>
  <tr><td>cell 3</td><td>cell 4</td></tr>
  <tr><td>cell 5</td><td>cell 6</td></tr>
</table>
```

Listing 7.4   A table with small cell borders and large cellpadding

Figure 7.4   Output of Listing 7.4

```
<table border="4" cellspacing="5" cellpadding="1">
  <tr><td>cell 1</td><td>cell 2</td></tr>
  <tr><td>cell 3</td><td>cell 4</td></tr>
  <tr><td>cell 5</td><td>cell 6</td></tr>
</table>
```

Listing 7.5   A table with large cell borders and small cellpadding

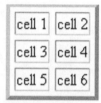

Figure 7.5   Output of Listing 7.5

Even if you don't include the border attribute, you can still define the cellspacing and cellpadding attributes. This will have the same spacing, but no lines in between the cells or around the table. In the example at the end of this topic (Listing 7.7), you will see an example using cellpadding without border.

Styling Your Data

Now that you have a basic understanding of HTML table structure, it is time to introduce some aesthetics. As mentioned in the introduction, CSS can be used to facilitate table positioning, orientation, and appearance. In fact, most common web pages use standard CSS elements for the header and for odd- and even-numbered rows. The alternating style layout creates a very easy to read table.

In the "Cascading Style Sheets" topic of Chapter 5, we introduced basic CSS and discussed how CSS classes can be used to aggregate a group of attributes as one or many classes. These classes can then be used to eliminate the need to add styles to every <table>, <tr>, or <td> tag individually.

Consider the following CSS (Listing 7.6), which defines style sets for <td>, <th>, and <table> tags, and creates a new version of our simple table:

```
<html>
<style>
td  { font: normal 8pt tahoma;
   text-align: center;
   background-color:darkkhaki; }
th  { font: bold 8pt tahoma;
   background-color:black;
   color:white;}
table  { border-color:black;
   border-style:solid;
      border-width:1;
width: 15%;}
.rowdark { background-color:darkkhaki }
.rowlight { background-color:khaki }
</style>
<body>
   <table id="table1" border="1">
      <tr><th>Simple Table</th></tr>
      <tr><td class="rowlight">File</td></tr>
      <tr><td class="rowdark">Edit</td></tr>
      <tr><td class="rowlight">View</td></tr>
      <tr><td class="rowdark">Project</td></tr>
   </table>
</body>
</html>
```

Listing 7.6   Styled HTML table

As you can see in Figure 7.6, these CSS style changes can greatly improve the look of your tables.

Note that we are applying a global CSS styling to <td>, <tr>, and <table> attributes. In addition to our global styles, we further apply our own rowdark and rowlight attributes to provide a ledger effect of alternating color bars. In the next topic, we will see a programmatic method for performing the alternating light and dark assignments.

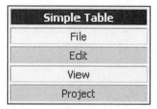

Figure 7.6   Applying styles to Figure 7.1

EXAMPLE

In this example, we will expand upon the simple table described in "How to Divide Your Screen" in Chapter 3 to include spacing within the table used for page layout. Notice that we use a larger number for the separation of cells in the layout table (cellpadding="6") versus the padding we use in the inner table storing e-mail information (cellpadding="2"). This creates a more obvious separation between the different parts of the web page (navigation, content, and header).

```
<html>
<!-- styles used for entire document -->
<style>
#TopHeader {text-align: center;}
#content {text-align: center;}
.rowdark { background-color:darkkhaki }
.rowlight { background-color:khaki }
</style>
<body>
<table width="100%" cellpadding="6">
<tr height="100" width="100%><td id="TopHeader"
    colspan="2">Employee's contact list</td></tr>
<tr>
  <td width="15%">Put links to other corporate info here</td>
<!-- main content goes here -->
  <td width="85%" id="content">
    <table cellpadding="2">
      <tr><th colspan="2">E-mail addresses</th></tr>
      <tr><td class="rowlight">Matt Jay</td>
        <td class="rowlight">mjjay@nocompany.com</td></tr>
      <tr><td class="rowdark">Nick Knez</td>
        <td class="rowdark">nknez@nowhere.com</td></tr>
```

```
    <tr><td class="rowlight">Matt Wilsack</td>
        <td class="rowlight">mwilsack@somewhere.com</td></tr>
  </table>
  </td>
</tr>
</table>
</body>
</html>
```

Listing 7.7   companyEmails.html

Also, notice for the e-mail addresses table shown in Figure 7.7 that we didn't use a border. Instead we used whitespace to separate the various cells in the table. This is always an alternative to using borders to separate the content—the decision to use borders or whitespace can be based on personal preference, as there is not a big difference in usability for whitespace versus lines.

Figure 7.7   Output of Listing 7.7

HOW AND WHY

Can I Create a Table within a Table?
Yes, you can create a table within a table. When using a table as an alternative to frames for page layout, as we did in the previous example (Listing 7.7), you will need to create a table within a table anytime you wish to include a table within the content section. A table must be included within a cell (<td> tags) of another table to be included within the table, as shown in Listing 7.8.

```
<table id="outer" border="2">
  <tr><td>cell 1</td><td>cell 2</td></tr>
  <tr><td>cell 3</td><td>cell 4</td></tr>
  <tr><td>
  <table id="inner" border="2">
    <tr><td>in cell 1</td><td>in cell 2</td></tr>
    <tr><td>in cell 3</td><td>in cell 4</td></tr>
  </table></td><td>cell 5</td></tr>
</table>
```

Listing 7.8   Tables within tables

As you can see from the output for this table (Figure 7.8), the entire table will be inserted within the single cell, and all other cells in the table will be resized accordingly.

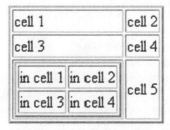

Figure 7.8   Output of Listing 7.8

What Happens When I Have Multiple Rows with Conflicting Numbers of Data Elements?
Given the <table> syntax, it is very easy to create rows with different numbers of columns. Listing 7.9, for example, creates one row with two columns and four rows with a single column:

```
<table border="1">
<tr><th>Simple Table</th></tr>
<tr><td>File</td><td>New</td></tr>
<tr><td>Edit</td></tr>
<tr><td>View</td></tr>
```

Listing 7.9   Conflicting row assignments

In the event of heterogeneous rows, the table will simply expand to the right, and attributes of the table (border type, color) will simply "shine through" around the extra column, as illustrated in Figure 7.9.

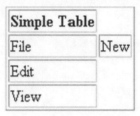

Figure 7.9   Ragged rows

Tables with ragged rows are not very appealing. You should always base your table on the row that requires the most cells. You can use the `colspan` attribute in the other rows to eliminate extra cells. However, simply adding a cell creates an uneven table. As an alternative, you can create a table within the table.

DESIGN NOTES

Implementing Tables with a WYSIWYG Application

Third-party applications such as Macromedia's Dreamweaver can be used quite effectively to generate tables. Dreamweaver is a WYSIWYG editor (which stands for "What You See Is What You Get," pronounced "wizzy-wig"). WYSIWYG applications let you design your web pages without the burden of hand-coding the HTML. These editors allow you to simply drag and drop images around a page, choose colors from a nice palate, or input text like a regular word processor. The nice part is that the HTML is generated for you.

The problem with the majority of these types of editors is that they tend to generate bulky code that makes the maintenance of a large website difficult. Newer products on the market, such as Dreamweaver 4.0, produce great tabular framework code. These graphical applications enable page layouts and tables that are easy to manipulate and use. Both

DHTML and JavaScript effects can be easily added through drag-and-drop tools. For an explanation on how to leverage Dreamweaver to produce tables, please consult the CodeNotes website ⊶🅒🅝UI070002.

Table Styling

In the previous example, we used alternating colors in a ledger effect to give our table a more eye-pleasing look. Referring to Chapter 3, you should keep the following rules in mind for your data tables:

1. Choose a background color that is less saturated than the text. A good idea is to use a monochromatic color scheme with different levels of saturation for alternating rows. You want to create some degree of contrast, but you don't want a loud, over-the-top color scheme.
2. Make sure your text is readable on the background. We used black text in Listing 7.6 because we're using a relatively light background color scheme. With large amounts of data it may also be desirable to have a small font size to reduce the amount of web space your table takes up. In our case, we've used a sans serif Tahoma 8-point font.

Of course, your tables should conform to your site's style constraints, but keeping these points in mind can promote an elegant tabular presentation.

SUMMARY

Basic HTML tables serve two distinct purposes: presenting tabular data and arranging HTML elements. When you are creating a table to display data, keep the following rules in mind:

1. Use three CSS styles to create a header with alternating rows. This style of data table has become very common on the Web and is very easy to read.
2. Avoid ragged edges. Either use colspan and rowspan to combine cells or insert a table within your table to organize space.
3. Use the border wisely. During your design phase, the border can help you trap errors and judge the amount of space you assign to a particular element. However, most web based tables use a very thin border (if any at all) during production. By careful use of CSS, you can create a readable table without the table border.
4. Use element spacing to create the illusion of a border. A 1- or

2-pixel padding between elements creates the illusion of a border and effectively separates table elements, without adding extra graphics and screen clutter.

The rules for using a table to lay out a web page are very similar; however, the CSS rules do not apply, and borders should be avoided.

Topic: Integrating Tables with DHTML/JavaScript

As with most HTML elements, table elements are accessible via the DOM. It is possible to change cells, rows, or the entire table dynamically, just as it is possible to write event-handling code to make tabled data interactive. By combining the DOM and JavaScript, we can create many common interactive table effects.

CONCEPTS

The mouseOver Highlight

One common and pleasing effect involving tables is the mouseOver highlight. This is where a particular cell changes its brightness, color, or border when the mouse is positioned over it. Although it is difficult to show in print, the result is something like that shown in Figure 7.10.

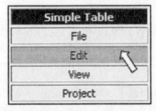

Figure 7.10   The mouseOver effect

The interactive effect shown in Figure 7.10 can be brought about by adding an event-handling function to the simple table from the previous topic:

```
<table>
<!--CSS omitted for brevity, similar to Listing 7.6 -->
<script>
```

```
function highlight(e, b)
{
  var src;
  // Fork for Netscape event handling
  if (navigator.appName == "Netscape")
    src = e.target;
  else
    src = e.srcElement;
  if (src.tagName == "TD")
  {
    if(b==true) //mouseOver, add highlight
    {
      src.origColor=src.style.backgroundColor;
      src.style.backgroundColor="darkkhaki";
    }
    else //mouseOut, restore original color
      src.style.backgroundColor=src.origColor;
  }
}
</script>
<body>
<table border="1" onmouseover="highlight(event,true)"
    onmouseout="highlight(event,false)">
  <!--table elements omitted for brevity,
      similar to Listing 7.6 -->
</table>
```

Listing 7.10   The mouseOver effect

Note that by placing the event handler in the attribute of the <table> element, we are taking advantage of event bubbling, discussed in the "Event Bubbling" section of Chapter 5. The mouseOver and mouseOut events really originate from the cells themselves. Rather than adding event handling to each <td> element, we simply capture the event and process it at the table level. In IE and Netscape 6.0, events bubble up from the originating element (cell to row to table), whereas in Netscape 4.x and earlier they trickle down to the triggering element (document to body to table). Either way, the <table> element handler will trap the event for every cell in the table.

Client-Side Sorting

One of the most commonly neglected, yet most commonly requested, data table features involves sorting. As users, we have come to expect that clicking on a table heading will automatically sort the table by that column of data. You can perform this sort easily using server-side code; however, you can avoid the round-trip by sorting on the client using DHTML.

Assuming we have the HTML and CSS of Listing 7.6, we can add sorting functionality by adding an event handler to the table header and creating a sort function:

```
<!-- Line numbers are for reference, remove to use the code -->
1:function sort_handler(sort_function)
2:{
3:   var tableArray = new Array();
4:   var tableRecords;
5:
6:   // Get a reference to our table node
7:   tableNode = document.getElementById('table1');
8:
9:   // Build our array with the children elements
10:   tableRecords = tableNode.getElementsByTagName('TR');
11:   for(i=0; i<tableRecords.length-1; i++)
12:   {
13:     tableArray[i] = new Object();
14:     //i+1 because we don't want to include
15:     //the header
16:     tableArray[i].cellData =
17:        tableRecords.item(i+1).childNodes[0].innerHTML;
18:   }
19:
20:   tableArray.sort(sort_function);
21:
22:   for (i=0; i<tableRecords.length -1; i++)
23:   {  //i+1 so we don't include the <th> header in the sort
24:     tableRecords.item(i+1).childNodes[0].innerHTML =
25:        tableArray[i].cellData;
26:   }
27:}
28:
29:function name_sort(a, b)
30:{
31:   if (a.cellData < b.cellData) return -1;
32:   if (a.cellData > b.cellData) return 1;
33:   else return 0;
```

```
34:
35:}
```

Listing 7.11   Client-side sorting

To kick off the sort, we would add a simple event handler to the "Simple Table" header:

```
<!-- From Listing 7.6 -->
    <tr><th onclick="sort_handler(name_sort)">
        Simple Table</th></tr>
```

Listing 7.12   Launching the sort

While it might seem like there is a lot going on in Listing 7.11, it is actually quite straightforward. We need to sort data and the JavaScript array object provides a convenient sort method that we can leverage. Therefore, we first create an array (line 3). After we use the DOM to retrieve all the table records in our table (line 10), we iterate through this collection (line 11), extract the data, and place it, element by element, in a new array, tableArray (lines 16–17).

Next, we sort the array (line 20). An array's sort() method takes a predicate as an argument. A predicate is simply a function that, when passed two values, indicates by its return value which is greater or lesser. If the return value is greater than 0, the first of the two elements is sorted to a higher index than the second. Similarly, if the return value is less than 0, the second element is sorted to a higher index than the first. If the return value is 0, the order of the two elements remains unchanged. In our case, the predicate is the name_sort() function.

After tableArray is sorted, we can iterate through tableRecords (line 22), replacing each record with the sorted records in tableArray using the innerHTML attribute. The table will now be sorted.

Generalizing Sorting to Multiple Columns
In the previous section, we demonstrated how to sort a single-column table. If you have multiple columns, the solution is only slightly more complex. To put it simply, we have to add an extra argument indicating the column and make sure to extract only the appropriate data from the table.

In lines 17 and 24 of Listing 7.11 you will notice that we are accessing a particular element of the tableArray, specifically, a childNode object. Remember that every element of the tableArray is a table record.

If you now recall that every table record may have one or more columns (<td> elements), you will not be surprised to find that the childNodes property of a table record will have as many elements as there are columns. Thus, if we were sorting a table that had two columns per row, the code would need to be rewritten and augmented only slightly to yield the following:

```
<!-- From Listing 7.11 -->
16: tableArray[i].cellData1 =
17:     tableRecords.item(i+1).childNodes[0].innerHTML;
18:
19: tableArray[i].cellData2 =
20:     tableRecords.item(i+1).childNodes[1].innerText;
```

Listing 7.13   Accessing the correct column

Additionally, one would need to account for the particular type of column we wished to sort on (i.e., numeric or character-based). Thus, the name_sort() function beginning at line 29 would need to be modified to sort on the correct column type. Since an array's sort() method may only take a two-argument predicate, you could use a global variable to select a particular column type, or you could create the predicate dynamically as discussed subsequently in "How Do I Dynamically Create a Predicate Function." The example in Listing 7.14 uses a global variable to determine the type of sort:

```
function sort(a, b)
{
  if (g_sortByAlpha)    // Sort by alphanumeric-character
  {
    if (a.cellAlphaData < b.cellAlphaData)
      return -1;
    if (a. cellAlphaData > b. cellAlphaData)
      return 1;
    else
      return 0;
  }
  else if (g_sortByNumeric)    // Sort by number
  {
    return (a.cellNumberData - b.cellNumberData);
  }
```

Listing 7.14   Conditional column-type sorting using a global variable

Note in this case that sorting numeric data is more straightforward than sorting character data. We simply subtract the two numbers, with the return value specifying the sorted order of the two elements.

Automating Row Styles

In the examples we have used so far, we have implemented a nice ledger-style color feature, whereby each row alternates between two colors. The JavaScript necessary to automate this task is quite simple. Assuming once again that we have a one-column, multiple-row table and the CSS defined in Listing 7.6, the formatCells() function shown in Listing 7.15 is all that is required.

```
function formatCells()
{  var tableNode;
   var x;
   tableNode = document.getElementById('table1');
   x = tableNode.getElementsByTagName('TR');
   for (i=1; i<x.length; i++)
   {
     if (i%2)
     {
       x.item(i).childNodes[0].className = "rowlight";
     }
   }
}
</script>
</HEAD>
<BODY onload="formatCells()">
<!--table HTML omitted for brevity -->
```

Listing 7.15 Automated row styles

Keep in mind that the table will already be homogeneously "darkkhaki" according to the CSS declarations. So the formatCells() function need only color every other row as "khaki" by applying the CSS class "rowlight" to alternating rows.

Last, note that functions attached to the <body> onload property will execute only after all HTML has been loaded.

EXAMPLE

The CodeNotes website contains a table example (and HTML code) for a rather complicated table that illustrates all of these effects ⊶CN⟶UI070003.

HOW AND WHY

How Do I Dynamically Create a Predicate Function?

As we discussed in the "Functions" section of Chapter 4, it is possible to create functions dynamically. Since predicate functions are simply a special type of function, it is possible to dynamically create predicate functions inside of the call to a sort method. In Listing 7.16, we outline the steps for dynamically creating a predicate function. Remember, the last argument to a function constructor is the function code, whereas the first parameters are the function parameters. Since predicates always accept only two parameters, you can use the same two parameter names for the parameters and then simply change the function code. If you cannot ensure that your code will use the same parameter names, you will have to use parameters to store the names of the parameters as well.

```
var functionCode;
/** in this section you would assign a value to functionCode.
  ie.
  functionCode = "if (x==y) {return 0;} else if (x>y) {return
      1;} else {return -1;}";
*/
sort_handler(new Function("x", "y", functionCode));
```

Listing 7.16   Creating a predicate function dynamically

How Can I Create a Table Using XML/XSLT?

Many of the aesthetic and interactive features we might want to imbue a table with are boilerplate code. Sorting, alternating color bars, mouseOver effects, and others generally require almost identical code, regardless of the size of the table or the data displayed. We can therefore leverage XML and XSLT to automatically generate the appropriate code (see Chapter 6). First, we have to ensure that our data is in XML form.

```
<?xml version="1.0"?>
<?xml-stylesheet type="text/xsl" href="table2html.xsl"?>
```

```
<menu>
  <header>Simple Table</header>
    <option>File</option>
    <option>Edit</option>
    <option>View</option>
    <option>Project</option>
</menu>
```

Listing 7.17   Table generation with XML

This XML document can be transformed into a table that supports the DHTML mouseOver event by using the following XSLT:

```
<?xml version="1.0" encoding="iso-8859-1"?>
<xsl:stylesheet version="1.0"
   xmlns:xsl="http://www.w3.org/1999/XSL/Transform">

<xsl:template match="/menu">
<html>
<head>
  <style>….</style>omitted for brevity
  <script>…</script>omitted for brevity
</head>
<body>

<table border="1" onmouseover="table_highlight(event, true)"
  onmouseout="table_highlight(event, false)">
  <tr>
    <xsl:for-each select="header">
      <th><xsl:value-of select="."/></th>
    </xsl:for-each>
  </tr>

  <xsl:for-each select="option">
    <tr>
    <td><xsl:value-of select="."/></td>
    </tr>
  </xsl:for-each>
</table>

</body>
</html>
```

```
</xsl:template>
</xsl:stylesheet>
```

Listing 7.18   Table generation XSLT transform

Admittedly, the XSL we have shown you is quite simple. But at
°^{CN}UI070004 you will find a gallery of more complex XSLT transforms
that will demonstrate far more complex transformations and yield interactive tables with any number of columns.

DESIGN NOTES

Accessing Data from an XML Recordset

Most enterprise applications use a relational database to store and retrieve tabular data. One widely used approach to extract this data is to
use a server-side query using some sort of middle-tier database connection object. A typical model using Microsoft's Active Server Pages
(ASP) for example, is to retrieve data using Active Data Objects (ADO)
and then add presentation-level HTML while looping through the
recordset. However, this model brings with it the unhealthy situation of
mixing presentation with data.

One of the advantages of using XML and XSLT for table representation is that it separates presentation from the data. The XML/XSLT approach can be used to convert the recordset into XML and apply an
XSLT transformation to produce HTML. In fact, some databases such as
SQL Server 2000 and Oracle have the capability of generating XML
recordsets directly. For example, you can leverage ASP to start an XML
conversion using a relational database, retrieve the recordset in the form
of XML, and stream the XML right into an ASP response object. Once
converted, you can use this XML with an XSLT stylesheet to complete
your tables, similar to our previous example. This model offers the advantages of extensibility and reusability, since you're eliminating the
mixing of code with HTML and you can reuse the XSL stylesheet on
any of your pages.

For more information, the CodeNotes website has examples of how to
access and display data from a relational database, using XML and XSLT
°^{CN}UI070005.

SUMMARY

This topic illustrated several of the more common effects used to make
an HTML table interactive. These standard effects have become ex-

pected features for most web users. Always keep in mind that your web-based tables will be compared to tables generated using dedicated spreadsheet programs such as Microsoft Excel. Even though you cannot (and shouldn't) duplicate all of the powerful spreadsheet features in your web tables, you should definitely provide common niceties, such as sorting, alternating colors, and mouseOver effects.

Chapter Summary

Keep in mind that tables serve two distinct, but related, purposes. First, a table can be used in its traditional form to display columns and rows of data. In a web-based GUI, you can leverage JavaScript, CSS, and the DOM to create data tables that are interactive, aesthetically colored, and formatted precisely to fit your data set. If possible, you can also leverage XML and XSL to automatically generate much of the boilerplate code required to sort columns, color alternate rows, and provide mouseOver highlights.

The second major purpose for tables is to organize your web page. Tables can be used to create a layout in which each element is properly aligned. By nesting tables within tables, you can create an almost infinite variety of patterns for your website. Keep in mind, however, that the largest element should always be used for content.

Chapter 8

—

TREES AND MENUS

A tree is an intuitive and effective way to display hierarchical data. Thus, trees are employed for many purposes in web and application UI: navigation menus, file hierarchies, site maps, and others. If you recall from Chapter 3, navigation is one of the most critical aspects of any website. Effectively using trees, therefore, is an integral part of designing an easily navigable website. The first topic in this chapter explains how to create common tree structures using HTML, DHTML, JavaScript, and CSS.

Menus, on the other hand, are more often found on desktop applications. If you are going to build menus into your web applications, you can leverage tables, DHTML, and JavaScript to create menus that are almost as friendly and usable as the standard menus found in most applications. The second topic in this chapter will show you the basic steps involved in creating menus for your web applications.

Whereas the previous chapters have focused on teaching fundamental concepts and basics of DHTML, JavaScript, and CSS, this chapter will focus on the application of these concepts to typical web navigation devices.

SIMPLE APPLICATION

A simple menu navigation bar can be generated with a table and some CSS styling:

```
<html>
<head>
<style>
  .header {font: normal 8pt tahoma;
           text-align: center;
           color: white;
           background-color: #006666;
           border:0px;}
</style>
</head>

<body>
  <table bgcolor="#006666" width="300px" border="0"
     cellpadding="0" cellspacing="0">
    <tr>
      <td class="header">File</td>
      <td class="header">Edit</td>
      <td class="header">Window</td>
      <td class="header">Help</td>
    </tr>
  </table>
</body>
</html>
```

Listing 8.1   Simple navigation bar HTML

This creates a bar at the top of the page that can be used as the basis for a menu, as shown in Figure 8.1.

Figure 8.1   Simple navigation bar

We will expand on this basic menu example throughout this chapter.

CORE CONCEPTS

Content or Navigation?

Trees and menus are used primarily to provide navigation links and actions. However, you should always keep in mind that trees and menus also serve as a place to display content. Simply by including items in a tree listing or menu, you automatically add importance to the item. If you recall from Chapter 3, no more than 20 percent of your web page should be devoted to navigation. However, you can cheat a little bit by using your navigation areas to display content. Your navigation tree, for example, can provide a web link (e.g., www.codenotes.com) or it can display information about the link (e.g., The CodeNotes Home Page . . . backed by the link).

Simple Navigation

If you use trees or menus for navigation, make sure that the main user patterns are easily accessible. For example, if most of your users access the "downloads" page, make sure the link to this page is at the top of the tree or at a high level in the menu. Keep the navigation paths as short as possible so that your users will spend time reading your content (or browsing your products), rather than navigating through a cumbersome menu structure or searching through a large, many-layered navigation tree.

Topic: Trees

The tree is a common way of storing and displaying data in a hierarchical manner. Trees can provide useful navigation features or simple displays of hierarchical data. Using basic HTML, you can create simple trees based on ordered and unordered lists. By nesting lists, you can add branches to your tree. These simple trees can be improved in many ways. Using DHTML, you can add simple event handlers that will make your tree collapsible. In addition, by using JavaScript and the DOM, you can create trees that are dynamically generated. All of these tree designs are illustrated in this topic.

CONCEPTS

Unordered Lists

Unordered lists use bullet points or some other icon to indicate individual items. An unordered list is defined using the <ul> tag, with an optional type attribute. The type attribute identifies the graphic that will be used for the particular list: circle, disc, or square. The default type is disc (a solid circle). Listing 8.2 illustrates a nested set of unordered lists using several different types of markers:

```
<h1>Corporate Directory</h1>
<ul>
<li>President
```

```
<ul type="square">
<li> AVP of Finance</li>
  <ul type="circle">
    <li> Finance Manager1</li>
    <li> Finance Manager2</li>
  </ul>
  <li> AVP of Sales</li>
  <ul type="disc">
  <li> Sales Manager</li>
    <ul type="disc">
    <li>Sales Clerk</li>
    </ul>
  </ul>
  <li> AVP of Consulting</li>
    <ul type="disc">
    <li>Consultant 1</li>
    <li>Consultant 2</li>
    </ul>
  </ul>
</ul>
```

Listing 8.2   simpletree.html

Individual list items are identified with <li> tags. These tags are also used in ordered lists. Rendering the HTML in Listing 8.2 results in Figure 8.2.

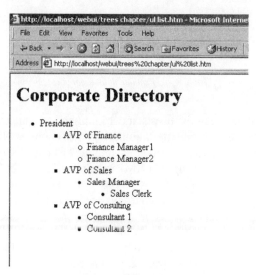

Figure 8.2   A simple list-based tree

Ordered Lists

Had we used `<ol>` (ordered list) in Listing 8.2, instead of `<ul>`, the browser would have automatically numbered the `<li>` entries. Specifically, `<ol type="A">` will provide automatic lettering of subelements A to Z, `<ol type="i">` provides Roman numerals, and `<ol type="1">` provides integer numbering. Not only can you put lists inside of lists, you can change the numbering type of the list, as illustrated in Listing 8.3.

```
<h1>CodeNotes UI</h1>
<ol>
<li>Intro</li>
  <ol type="A">
    <li>Orientation</li>
    <li>History</li>
    <li>Background</li>
  </ol>
<li>Installation</li>
  <ol type="i">
    <li>Browser Version</li>
    <li>Current Releases</li>
  </ol>
<li> User Interface Design Theory </li>
  <ol type="1">
    <li>Core Concepts</li>
    <li>Navigation</li>
    <li>Colors</li>
  </ol>
</ol>
```

Listing 8.3   Example of an ordered list

Notice that the main list uses standard numbering (integers), the first sublist (Intro) uses capital letter numbering, the second sublist (Installation) uses lowercase Roman numerals, and the last list uses integer numbering explicitly. Rendering this XML results in the tree in Figure 8.3.

If you want, you can even nest unordered lists in ordered lists, and vice versa. Just make sure that your tags are in the proper order.

Collapsible Trees

Trees with many nested levels can be rather long and difficult to navigate. In general, such nested trees are made collapsible, so that subtrees can be expanded on demand. By adding a small amount of DHTML to a

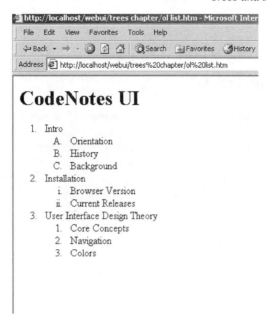

Figure 8.3   Various types of ordered lists

tree, nodes of the tree can be made to expand and collapse branches when clicked. Listing 8.4 contains several CSS definitions and inserts an event handler into the main tree nodes.

```
<HTML>
<!-- This example requires three graphics:  plus.gif, minus.gif
and item.gif.  See CN⇒UI080001 for these graphics, or use your
own -->

<!-- CSS definitions -->
<style>
  .header {
    cursor:hand;
    font-family:Arial,sans-serif;
    font-size: x-small;
    font-weight:bold;
    list-style-image:url(plus.gif)
  }
  .item {
    list-style-image:url(item.gif)
  }
</style>
```

```
<!-- Insert Listing 8.5 here -->

<!-- Build Tree -->
<body>
<h1>CodeNotes UI</h1>
<ol>
  <li onclick="menuAction(event, 'menu1')" class="header">
    Intro</li>
  <ol id="menu1" style="display:none" type="A">
    <li class="item">Orientation</li>
    <li class="item"> History</li>
    <li class="item">Background</li>
  </ol>
  <li onclick="menuAction(event, 'menu2')" class="header">
    Installation</li>
  <ol id="menu2" style="display:none" type="i">
    <li class="item">Browser Version</li>
    <li class="item">Current Releases</li>
  </ol>
  <li onclick="menuAction(event, 'menu3')" class="header">
    User Interface Design Theory</li>
  <ol id="menu3" style="display:none" type="1">
    <li class="item">Core Concepts</li>
    <li class="item">Navigation</li>
    <li class="item">Colors</li>
  </ol>
</ol>
</body>
</HTML>
```

Listing 8.4   Collapsible tree HTML

In essence, we have a static ordered list that uses a separate CSS style (see "Cascading Style Sheets" topic, Chapter 5) for top-level menu items (header) and nested menu items (item). Each top-level menu item also has an event handler for onClick (see "Event Handlers" topic, Chapter 5). This handler calls the menuAction function, which is defined in Listing 8.5. Before we explore how the menuAction function expands and collapses branches of the tree, first note that we are leveraging the ordered list's style attribute, which exposes, among other things, the display value of an element. This display value can be manipulated to make the element seem to appear and disappear. The important settings for the display property are "none," "block," and "inline." Block elements begin on a new line (useful for lists), while "inline" simply adds the target element in line with its surrounding elements.

The `menuAction` function, shown next in Listing 8.5, leverages the `display` property and the DOM to make our tree collapsible and expandable:

```
<!-- Insert into Listing 8.4 -->
<script>
function menuAction(e, objID)
{
  var src;
  var obj;

  // Fork for Netscape event handling
  if (navigator.appName == "Netscape")
    src = e.target;
  else
    src = e.srcElement;

  //Showing and hiding branches only applies to headers. We can
  //simply check the CSS style to see if we have a "header"
  if (src.className == "header")
  {
    obj = document.getElementById(objID);
    if (obj.style.display=="none")
    {
      obj.style.display="block";
      obj.style.listStyleImage="url(minus.gif)";
    }
    else
    {
      obj.style.display="none";
      obj.style.listStyleImage="url(plus.gif)";
    }
  }
}
</script>
```

Listing 8.5   Collapsible tree JavaScript

The JavaScript in Listing 8.5 is fairly straightforward: if you click a header with a "plus" graphic beside it, its style will be set to "list-items," its children will appear underneath, and it will be given a "minus" icon.

These and other GIF files used in this CodeNote may be found at
o^{CN}UI080001. Listing 8.5 will produce a web page similar to that shown
in Figure 8.3, but will be interactively expandable and collapsible.

Dynamic Trees

In the previous example, Listing 8.5, we added JavaScript to a static ordered list, giving it the ability to expand and collapse its branches. It is
often the case, however, that the children of a particular node of a tree
are not known until the moment parent node is clicked. In other words,
we must sometimes construct branches of our tree on the fly. This behavior is also quite common when a tree is very large. Top-level items
are loaded at start-up, but lower-level items are only loaded on demand.
By only loading the top-level items at start-up, the page appears faster.
The example later in this topic illustrates a fully dynamic tree.

Using the <div> and <span> tags

Div and span tags are used as container elements for holding data. You
can encapsulate one or more elements, such as a group of paragraphs,
inside a div or span tag, allowing the enclosed element(s) to inherit the
properties of the parent div/span tag. This grouping is useful for applying a single style to a block of enclosed elements. For example, you
could use a div in conjunction with CSS to apply a specific style to a
section of your page inside your div tag. Or you could set the display
style attribute of a page block enclosed within a div dynamically to
make the entire collection of elements visible or hidden.

Div tags cause a line break <br> before and after the div element,
whereas span tags do not. Because span tags do not insert a line break,
span tags are used more for in-line positioning, when effects are desired
in the normal flow of texts and images. The next examples make use of
the div and span tags.

EXAMPLE

If you recall the DOM tree presented at the beginning of Chapter 6, you
might remember that the DOM is essentially a tree-like hierarchy of objects and attributes. In the following example, we demonstrate how to iterate through the DOM hierarchy using a collapsible, dynamically
generated tree structure. The full code for this example is too long for
this format; however, it is available on the CodeNotes website at
o^{CN}UI080002.

The DOM Tree

The top-level node (or root node) in our particular tree will be a DOM window object. Clicking this object will open a branch containing all the children of the window object. If a child is an object, it will have the same icon as the window object (a folder). If the child is a property or method, it will have a different image (a page). The DOM Explorer Tree is shown in Figure 8.4.

Figure 8.4   DOM Explorer

Base HTML

The HTML for the DOM Explorer Tree is very straightforward, and it is shown in Listing 8.6.

```
<html>
<!-- Example uses folderminus.gif, folderplus.gif.  See
UI080001 or use your own icons -->
```

```
<script>
  // Add javascript for DisplayChildren event here
  // Listing 8.7, Listing 8.8, and Listing 8.9
</script>
<body>
<ul>
  <li class='header' onClick="displayChildren(event,
    window, 'window')"> Window </li>
</ul>
</body>
</html>
```

Listing 8.6   DOM Explorer HTML

You will notice that we begin with an unordered list with a single list item: the window object. The onClick handler for this item calls the displayChildren function.

The displayChildren Function
The displayChildren function uses standard JavaScript; however, it is rather complicated. Listing 8.7 provides the basic framework:

```
function displayChildren(e, obj, parentName)
{
  try
  {
    var src;

    // stop event bubbling
    e.cancelBubble = true;

    // Determine what browser we're using
    if (navigator.appName == "Netscape")
      src = e.target;
    else
      src = e.srcElement;

    // Return if we've clicked on an attribute
    if (src.className == 'item') {return;}

    //Show or build sub-tree (Listing 8.8 and 8.9)
    if (src.isDirty=='true')
    {
```

```
      showBranch(src);
    }
    else
    {
      makeBranch(src);
    }
  }
  catch(error)
  {
    alert("Object not supported by this browser");
  }
}
```

Listing 8.7   DOM Explorer JavaScript

The displayChildren function operates on a simple principle. When an object is clicked, the function dynamically builds new list item elements and injects them dynamically into the tree via the clicked object's innerHTML property. Thus, the tree builds itself as the user navigates it. The framework in Listing 8.7 creates some initial variables, handles the event, and traps for the condition when a user clicks on an item that does not have any children (e.g., an attribute). If the user clicks on a regular item, either showBranch or makeBranch is called, depending on whether the branch already exists. Both functions are explained in the following sections.

The makeBranch Function
When the user clicks on an item, a new subbranch is created, containing all of the item's child elements. The makeBranch function (Listing 8.8) creates this new subtree by using a for..in construct to iterate through every property of the selected item. If the property is an object, it is added to folderArray. If the property is not an object, it is added to the itemArray. The arrays are sorted, and then a new innerHTML string is created and added to the root item.

```
function makeBranch(obj)
{
  var prop;
  var HTMLStr = new String();
  var folderArray = new Array();
  var itemArray = new Array();
  var folderIndex = 0;
  var itemIndex = 0;
  // Iterate through all properties of this particular object
```

```
for (prop in obj)
{
  if ((obj[prop] != null) && (typeof(obj[prop]) == "object"))
    folderArray[folderIndex++] = prop;
  else
    itemArray[itemIndex++] = prop;
}
// Sort our arrays
folderArray.sort();
itemArray.sort();
// Build our HTML string.
HTMLStr = "<ul>";
for (i=0; i < folderArray.length; i++)
{
  HTMLStr += genFolderString(parentName, folderArray[i]);
}
for (i=0; i < itemArray.length; i++)
{
  HTMLStr += genItemString(parentName, itemArray[i]);
}
HTMLStr += "</ul>";
// Create our element to append to our tree.
x = document.createElement('DIV');
x.innerHTML = HTMLStr;
// Finally, add to our tree
src.appendChild(x);
src.isDirty = true;
src.style.listStyleImage="url(folderminus.gif)";
}
```

Listing 8.8   The makeBranch function

The genItemString and genFolderString methods (not shown) create new <li> tags for each subitem. These strings are added to the HTMLStr variable. Because we sorted folderArray and itemArray before generating the list, the items are grouped by type and sorted within type. In other words, the sorted objects are displayed before the sorted attributes. Both types of objects are tied into a <div> tag so that we can apply the same formatting to all tags simultaneously.

The string generated by genFolderString also contains HTML for an onClick event handler (one for each object in the new branch so we can click on the new object and expand it), as well as information about the parent node it is associated with.

The showBranch Function

Because building a new branch is a relatively costly operation and the subbranches do not change during the user session, we want to cache the tree information. In other words, we don't want to rebuild a submenu every time the user clicks on a node. If the menu is already there, we simply want to display it. We determine whether or not a branch has been built by using the isDirty property, which we declare as an attribute of each branch. After a branch has been built, we can simply check to see if the isDirty property is true and set its display property accordingly ("none" to hide it or "block" to show it).

```
function showBranch(src) {
  // The hierarchy we're iterating through is in the form:
  // <LI><text><DIV>
  // We need to iterate down a level, and across a sibling
  if (src.firstChild.nextSibling.style.display == "none")
  {
    src.firstChild.nextSibling.style.display = "block";
    src.style.listStyleImage="url(folderminus.gif)";
  }
  else
  {
    src.firstChild.nextSibling.style.display = "none";
    src.style.listStyleImage="url(folderplus.gif)";
  }
}
```

Listing 8.9   The showBranch function

To access the node we want to expand, we have to iterate down a child and across a sibling (as shown in bold in Listing 8.9. This is because we have a text node (representing the text header) between our <li> tag and our target <div> tag, as shown in Figure 8.5.

Once again, you can obtain a downloadable version of the DOM Explorer from the CodeNotes website °C⁄>UI080002.

HOW AND WHY

Can I Use Collapsible Trees in Frames?

You can use collapsible trees in a frame; however, the tree may expand out of the available space. Trees typically expand to the right, so if you are using a small column as your frame, it may expand outside the bor-

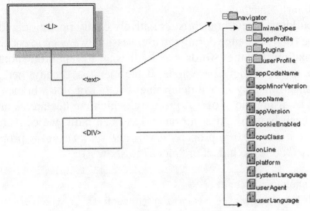

Figure 8.5   DOM Explorer node hierarchy

ders you've set. Make sure you have scrolling set to "yes" or "auto" in your frame tag.

```
<frame src='myframe.html' scrolling='auto'>
```

Listing 8.10   Using trees in a frame

Note, however, that most users will find having to scroll horizontally extremely annoying. Wherever possible, try to design your tree branches so that they are brief enough that they can't expand beyond the frame, or provide a frameless page to which users can go if they don't want to run into complications.

DESIGN NOTES

Using the Display and Visibility Style Properties
The previous section described some examples where we managed to make objects appear and disappear on the page, even after the page had been loaded. To do this we used the display style property.

Those familiar with CSS will know that there is a visibility property, as well as a display property. The difference between the two lies in the application of each property. The visibility property can be set to either "hidden" or "visible." The display property can be set to, among other things, "none," "block," or "inline."

If an element's display is set to "none", the space around the element collapses. The object appears to be taken out of the page flow. In contrast, when an element's visibility is set to "hidden", the invisible element still uses space on the page. If we had therefore used the visibility property instead of the display property in our preliminary tree example, we would have had whitespace between each top-level header.

You should use the visibility style property when you want to reserve space on the page for a hidden object. This can be useful for setting aside a page section to update on a mouse-over or on a toggled setting. You may, for example, want form elements to appear only if the user has entered certain input. The display style property, on the other hand, is useful for freeing space when an object is invisible. The surround objects are rearranged as if the hidden object weren't there. Knowing which style property to use is an important aspect of UI design.

Browser Differences

It is important to understand the subtle differences between how Netscape and IE represent tree nodes. If you want to, for example, iterate through a parent-child relationship, there are nodes you may not realize are there. Netscape treats all whitespace between elements in an HTML document as an extra node. IE does not. Therefore, you should try to eliminate whitespace between tags so as to make your code cross-browser compatible.

Additionally, IE 5.5 and Netscape 6.0 differ on their implementation of the root node. The root node of a page is technically the document object. However, the document object itself is not supported well by IE 5+. If you want to obtain a starting iteration point that is compatible with both browsers, you must use the document.documentElement node (which is the first and only child of the document object), as shown in Figure 8.6.

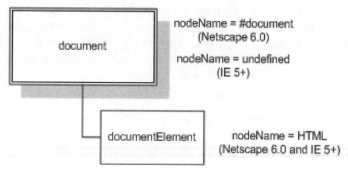

Figure 8.6   Root node hierarchy

SUMMARY

As stated at the beginning of this chapter, a tree—or any hierarchical structure, for that matter—can be used to make the end user's navigation experience more intuitive, while freeing the web space from clutter. Knowing when to implement a hierarchical structure, however, is just as important as knowing how to design it.

Referring to Chapter 3, keep in mind that the purpose of a hierarchy is to simplify data structures and navigation. Let users start with the major top-level components, find the one they want, and navigate down to a more specific sublevel. Use a tree when you have obvious parent-child or container relationships.

Use collapsible tree structures to save space on your web page. However, remember the two-click rule. If your tree extends beyond two levels, you might want to reconsider how the tree is arranged or provide alternative navigation tools such as a search feature. Similarly, building tree submenus on the fly can make your initial load time much faster. However, users may complain at the additional delay when menu items are selected. If a subitem is used regularly, it should be loaded at start-up.

Topic: Menus

Web-based GUIs have a number of intrinsic features, capabilities, and advantages that traditional nonweb GUIs don't. However, HTML does not define a specification for the cascading, drop-down style menus that adorn almost every application we use on our PCs. Applications such as Microsoft Word, Excel, Adobe Photoshop, and even our browsers themselves have convenient drop-down menus that allow us to set preferences, access files, purge caches, and so on. There is, unfortunately, no simple way to add a drop-down menu to an HTML page. With some clever use of DHTML/CSS, JavaScript, and tables, we can nonetheless imbue our pages with sophisticated menus.

CONCEPTS

Table-Based Drop-Down Menus

When creating an HTML menu, it is both intuitive and practical to design it as a single table that contains a grouping of other tables. Specifically, you can make every top-level menu item a table and every sub-menu under that specific topic a table record. Your "menu" would, at this point, simply appear as shown in Figure 8.7.

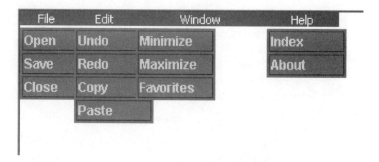

Figure 8.7   A menu laid out as a group of tables

The HTML for producing Figure 8.7 is shown in Listing 8.11.

```
<style>
  .header
   {
     font: normal 8pt tahoma;
     text-align: center;
     color: white;
     background-color: #006666;
     border:0px;
   }
  .menu
   {
     width:75px;
     border-color: #333366;
     color: #FFCC99;
     background-color: #666699;
   }
  td
   {
     font: Bold 12px Arial, Helvetica;
     color: #FFCC99;
     border:1px outset #663399;
   }
</style>
</head>
```

```
<body marginwidth="0" marginheight="0" style="margin: 0" >
  <table bgcolor="#006666" width="300px" border="0"
      cellpadding="0" cellspacing="0">
    <tr>
      <td  class="header">File
        <div style="position:absolute; visibility:hidden">
          <table class="menu">
            <tr><td>Open</td></tr>
            <tr><td>Save</td></tr>
            <tr><td>Close</td></tr>
          </table>
        </div>
      </td>
      <td  class="header">Edit
        <div style="position:absolute; visibility:hidden">
          <table class="menu">
            <tr><td>Undo</td></tr>
            <tr><td>Redo</td></tr>
            <tr><td>Copy</td></tr>
            <tr><td>Paste</td></tr>
          </table>
        </div>
      </td>
<!-- Window and Help sub-menus are not shown here to
conserve space. See ᶜᴺ⇨UI080003 for complete source code -->

    </tr>
  </table>
</body>
</html>
```

Listing 8.11   A simple menu

Listing 8.11 should not contain many surprises. In essence, we have one master table containing one master row. The columns of this row are the top-level menu items (File, Edit, Window, and Help). Each column/top-level menu, however, itself contains a complete table where the rows represent the submenu items (e.g., for File we have Open, Save, Close, etc.). You will notice that the submenu tables are contained within a divider (<div>) element. We will see shortly, that the <div> element exists solely as a convenience, providing us with a way to group an entire series of elements (in this case, an entire table) into one element that styles may be applied to. By grouping a submenu/table as a <div>, we can apply visible and nonvisible styles (show and hide) to the

<div> itself, thus allowing our menus to appear when a mouse is moved over them and disappear when the mouse is moved away.

Adding the mouseOver Handler

When the HTML of Listing 8.11 is rendered by a browser, we will see only the top-level menu items (all the submenus are wrapped in a <div> whose style is set to "visibility:hidden"). We would like for the sub-menus to pop up when the mouse is moved over the top-level menu item. Thus, we need to tie a function, menu_action(), to the onMouseOver event handler that will make the submenu visible by changing the style of its containing <div> to "visible." Thus, HTML for the top-level menu items becomes:

```
<td onMouseOver="menu_action(this, true)"
onMouseOut="menu_action(this, false)" class="header">File
```

Listing 8.12   Dynamic visibility

The menu_action function is shown next in Listing 8.13. Note the JavaScript (line 24) that makes the submenu visible. Further explanation of the surrounding code follows this listing.

```
1:function menu_action(src, showMenu)
2:{
3:  if (showMenu == true)
4:  {
5:    // Clear our timer
6:    window.clearTimeout(popTimer);
7:    // Check to see if we have a menu waiting to
9:    //  be hidden
10:   if ((g_oldMenu != null))
11:   {
12:       close_menu();
13:   }
14:
15:   src.origColor=src.style.backgroundColor;
16:   src.style.backgroundColor="#669999";
17:
18:   // Pop up the new menu
19:   // Our hierarchy is <TD>
20:   //                     <text>
21:   //                  <div>
22:
23:   var menu = src.firstChild.nextSibling;
```

```
24:    menu.style.visibility = "visible";
25:    menu.style.left = src.offsetLeft;
26:    menu.style.top = (src.offsetTop +
27:      src.offsetHeight + 2);
28:  }
29:  else
30:  {
31:    // Set up our timer for closing this menu
32:    g_oldMenu = src;
33:    g_popTimer = window.setTimeout('close_menu()',
34:      400);
35:  }
36:}
```

Listing 8.13   The showMenu function

Line 3 evaluates the showMenu argument, which indicates whether the event handler "wishes" that a menu be displayed or not. Assume a value of true, and (ignoring lines 6–14 for the moment; we will discuss timeouts shortly) we see that lines 15 and 16 will provide a simple highlight effect on the top-level menu (it makes the color of the selected top level a lighter shade of green). Lines 23–27 make the submenu actually pop up. Since the src is an object reference to our top-level menu item (which is, itself, just a column of the master table), we need to navigate downward from the top-level menu item, to its text (e.g., File) and then one sibling at the same level, which will bring us to the <div>. We now have a reference to our submenu, so we place it in the variable called menu and apply a "visible" style (line 24) to our submenu and voila!: the submenu pops up.

We almost have a complete menu system. As you will see in the next section, we now need to consider the timing of the menu's appearance and disappearance for the illusion to be complete.

Menu Timeouts
If you examine lines 33–34 of Listing 8.13, you will notice that the window object's setTimeout method is being called. The setTimeout method registers a timed action with the window. This event will occur in the specified number of milliseconds. In Listing 8.13, we tell the window to execute the close_menu in 400 milliseconds. In other words, when the user moves away from a top-level menu item, the submenu will disappear (be made hidden) in roughly half a second.

The reason we need to introduce a delay is so that the cursor has time to cross a tiny bit of whitespace between the top-level menu item and a submenu item. In other words, if a user selects File and File's submenu pops up, the user needs to cross a little bit of whitespace to reach Edit. If there is no timeout, the submenu will close before the user can reach the menu item. You can try various timeout settings; however, 400 milliseconds is fairly standard.

If you are wondering where this whitespace comes from, you can think of it coming from a few different places. If you examine lines 26 and 27, you will notice that we are introducing a couple of pixels between the submenu and the top-level menu for aesthetic reasons. However, even if we eliminated this small gap, a top-level column/menu item may be wider than its submenu. If you examine Figure 8.7, you will notice that Window is wider than its submenu; therefore, if Window was highlighted, but the mouse was in the far right corner of the Window column, a diagonal path to the submenu would take it through whitespace. Any path through whitespace or outside of the top-level menu items cell results in a mouseOut event being fired. Fortunately, after the mouseOut handler is called (menu_action(this, false)) the submenu will remain open and the cursor will have 400 milliseconds to make it to a submenu. As we will see in the next section, the submenu itself has a mouseOver handler whose handling function will clear the timer once you have highlighted a submenu item.

EXAMPLE

We hope you now understand the purpose of the timeout. We have taken a look at how the menu_action function shows and hides the submenus. We can now add a little more detail to the HTML of Listing 8.11 and add some event handlers.

```html
<table bgcolor"#006666" width="300px" border="0"
       cellpadding="0" cellspacing="0">
  <tr>
    <td onmouseover="menu_action(this, true)"
        onmouseout="menu_action(this, false)"
        class="header">File
      <div style="position:absolute; visibility:hidden">
        <table onmouseover="highlight_menu(event, true)"
           onmouseout="highlight_menu(event, false)"
           class="menu">
          <tr><td>Open</td></tr>
          <tr><td>Save</td></tr>
```

```
        <tr><td>Close</td></tr>
      </table>
    </div>
  </td>
  <td onmouseover="menu_action(this, true)"
      onmouseout="menu_action(this, false)"
      class="header">Edit
    <div style="position:absolute; visibility:hidden">
      <table onmouseover="highlight_menu(event, true)"
             onmouseout="highlight_menu(event, false)"
             class="menu">
        <tr><td>Undo</td></tr>
        <tr><td>Redo</td></tr>
        <tr><td>Copy</td></tr>
        <tr><td>Paste</td></tr>
      </table>
    </div>
  </td>
<!--remaining menus omitted for brevity, but they follow the
same pattern -->
```

Listing 8.14   The revised menu

From Listing 8.14 it should be apparent that when the mouse is moved over the top-level menu items, the menu_action function is called, which, as we have seen, makes the submenus visible or invisible in the case of mouseOver and mouseOut, respectively.

You will also notice that when the user moves the mouse over any of the submenu-items, the event will bubble up to the table where highlight_menu is called. As discussed in the previous section, highlight_menu will provide a highlighting effect and will "turn off" the timer so that the submenu does not disappear. The JavaScript for highlight_menu is shown in Listing 8.15.

```
function highlight_menu(e, highlight)
{
  var src;
  // Fork for Netscape event handling
  if (navigator.appName == "Netscape")
    src = event_obj.target;
  else
    src = event_obj.srcElement;
```

```
//we don't want the event bubbling up to the top-level
//menu-item because it has its own mouseOut and mouseOver
//handlers that perform different actions
e.cancelBubble = true;

if ((src.tagName == "TD") || (src.nodeName == "#text"))
{
  if (highlight == true)
  {
    //don't close the sub-menu
    //the user is highlighting a menu item
    window.clearTimeout(popTimer);
    src.origColor=src.style.backgroundColor;
    src.style.backgroundColor="#333366";
  }
  else
  {
    //it is a mouseOut, so put in a delayed
    //request to close the pop-up.  The user
    //still has 400ms to touch another menu
    //item.
    g_popTimer = window.setTimeout('close_menu()', 400);
    src.style.backgroundColor=src.origColor;
  }
}
}
```

Listing 8.15   The highlight_menu function

The full listing for this example can be found on the CodeNotes website at °CN UI080004.

HOW AND WHY

I've Used <menu> and <dir> Tags to Represent My Menu Schemes in the Past. What Happened to These Tags?
HTML 4.0 has deprecated the use of the <menu> and <dir> tags, which are both replaced by the <ul> (unordered list) tags. The functionality of both tags was essentially the same as <ul>. <menu> was intended for single words or very short phrases (a typical menu), while <dir> was sup-

posed to represent a directory list of computer files or programs (single-line names).

Menu-Building Tools

There are many third-party tools that you can download to design your own DHTML menus, without having to know anything about JavaScript or DHTML. These graphical applications can be used to readily speed up the design process. Microsoft offers a DHTML Tree Menu Builder, available on its MSDN website, while XFSJumpStart offers a very nice automatic menu-builder application. Links to these sites can be found on the CodeNotes website at ☚UI080005. The disadvantage of these applications is that you have obviously very limited control over the code base. But it may be worth considering if you want a quick and easy solution to implementing a dynamic client-side menu.

SUMMARY

Like the trees discussed in the first part of this chapter, menus serve to bring organization to a web page. We have chosen to show a static, collapsible menu as an example, because it is something end users will have certainly seen before. Remember, a good UI principle is to use conventions that are familiar to end users.

The problem with implementing a DHTML menu scheme, however, is that your code base is inevitably going to bulk up. Putting your menu functions in a JavaScript library file will help, but is it worth the complications of trying to develop your own menu? Enterprise solutions commonly require a central theme to your menu and you will want something that is easy to develop and that performs well. Adding items to the menu can sometimes be convoluted and inefficient, as it may involve searching through hundreds of lines of HTML.

Chapter Summary

Trees and menus can improve your web page by consolidating navigation features. Remember to use common conventions and conserve space. Also keep the two-click rule in mind. If your menus or trees require more than two clicks to navigate to the appropriate page, you should simplify your design. If you can't simplify your design, make sure that the most frequently accessed features are prominent in the tree or menu. In other words, use these tools to make your users' lives easier. Complicated menus and extensive tree structures can frustrate users and make navigation of your site very difficult.

APPENDIX

This section serves to outline the major differences between Internet Explorer and Netscape, as well as to provide a history of web technologies, including DOM, CSS, JavaScript, and HTML. A browser compatibility table and browser history timeline are presented at the end of the chapter. This chapter deviates from the format of the rest of the book and is intended to provide a useful reference for tackling browser compatibility issues. However, the information presented in this chapter should not be used as a substitute for browser-specific testing.

Document Object Model

WHAT IS DOM LEVEL 1?

The DOM Level 1 was published in October 1998 by the World Wide Web Consortium (www.w3c.org). It is defined in two parts: DOM Level 1 Core and DOM Level 1 HTML.

The DOM core is a set of low-level fundamental interfaces that can represent any structured document. In general, it represents any functionality required to manipulate hierarchical document structures, elements, or attributes. An example would be a `node`, `parent`, and `children` interface. In addition, it includes the notion of a node's `tag-names` and `attributes`, as discussed in Chapter 5.

The HTML-specific DOM API extends the Core API by providing a higher-level set of interfaces for common HTML objects such as input or text-area interfaces. The HTML DOM inherits all of the functionality of the core DOM.

WHAT IS DOM LEVEL 2?

The DOM Level 2 is a working draft specification that was last published by the W3C in November 2000. It represents an extension of the DOM core, as well as the introduction of several new models, including the View, Event, Style, and Traversal/Range models. These models provide additional functionality for manipulating HTML and creating responsive web pages.

Both Netscape 6.0 and IE 5.5 claim partial support for Level 2. These claims refer to specific interfaces not included in either the HTML or the Core DOM Level 1 specification. For example, the DOM Level 2 Event Model specifies a standardized way of handling events. This model includes things like event flow, event bubbling (discussed in Chapter 5), event-listener registration, and event interface type. Netscape's event object is significantly different from IE's (as discussed in the "Event Bubbling" concept of the "Event Handlers" topic in Chapter 5) and actually conforms more closely to the Level 2 DOM. Netscape, for example, specifies the W3C-compliant target property of an event. IE implements the property srcElement instead.

WHAT IS DOM LEVEL 3?

The DOM Level 3 is a working draft that was last published by the W3C in June 2001. Level 3 is very much in its infancy and has not as yet been implemented by IE or Netscape. Changes in Level 3 include the concept of Abstract Schemas (thus providing a representation for DTDs and XML Schemas), and DOM Load and Safe specifications (a standard API for loading XML source documents into a DOM representation), as well as expanding on the Event Model implemented in Level 2.

KEY RELEASE POINTS

Versions of IE Earlier Than 5.0 and Versions of Netscape Earlier Than 6.0 Have Significantly Different DOMs
If you are developing applications that must be compatible with earlier Netscape versions (4.x), you will in all likelihood have to fork your

code, or use an XML/XSLT translation scheme as specified in Chapter 6, when accessing the DOM methods and attributes. See "Using the Navigator Property for Browser Detection" in "The Document Object Model" topic of Chapter 5, and Chapter 6 ("XML/XSLT"), for an explanation of how to do this.

Versions of IE Earlier Than 4.0 and Versions of Netscape Earlier Than 4.x Do Not Support DHTML

IE 4.0 was a major release for Microsoft. It propelled Microsoft's browser far ahead of Netscape's Navigator in terms of its scripting abilities at the time and its capacity for instant page refreshing when content changed. Most significant, every visible element had the ability to be scripted via DHTML. Furthermore, IE's version of DHTML had a straightforward way of accessing the components of a page via the collection document.all, which was arguably simpler than Netscape's layers (eventually to be abandoned by Netscape with the release of Netscape 6.0.) For an explanation of Netscape's layers, see "Netscape Layers and the DOM" later in this appendix.

Netscape and IE Currently Implement Different Versions of the Event Interface

IE's event object is a child of the window object and therefore is globally accessible from JavaScript. Netscape's event object is not a global object, but is passed automatically as the first parameter in an event handler. See the design notes in the "Event Handlers" topic of Chapter 5 for more details.

RECENT RELEASES

Netscape and Microsoft have recently made a conscious effort to adhere to the W3C's Level 1 DOM standard. Both Netscape's 6.0 and Microsoft's IE 5+ are significant improvements in terms of embracing the W3C's specifications. However, there is still some confusion among developers about whether particular browsers support particular aspects of the specifications. Microsoft has historically neglected standards in favor of adding value using their own components (their widely used innerHTML attribute is a good example of this). Netscape felt that this feature was useful enough that they implemented it themselves with their version 6.0 browser.

Even though both Netscape and Microsoft have adopted a standard set by a standardizing body, each vendor has also added custom functionality on top, to differentiate their browsers from one another. Fortunately, with both browsers recognizing the W3C's DOM Level 1, developers can design with at least a common base standard.

At the time of this publication, Netscape 6.0 has the closest W3C Level 1 standard support (IE 6.0 should, however, place Microsoft at least in line with Netscape). This is not to say one browser is better than the other—just that one conforms more to the set of W3C standards.

IE's version 6.0, in beta testing at the time of writing, supposedly rounds out their DOM Level 1 support with the addition of some missing API methods. The additional methods center around support for attribute nodes that were missing in IE 5.5: `getAttributeNode`, `setAttributeNode`, and `createAttribute`. IE 5.5 supports most of DOM Level 1, with weak support for DOM Level 2.

Netscape 6.0 incorporates all of the DOM Level 1, and provides partial support for DOM level 2.

See Table A.2 for a high-level overview of the features supported by each browser type.

NETSCAPE LAYERS AND THE DOM

Netscape Layers were introduced with Netscape 4.x. They are implemented with the `<layer>` tag, and are analogous to a `<div>` or `<span>` tag, discussed in the "Trees" topic of Chapter 8. However, `<layer>` tags were never recognized by the W3C as a part of HTML and have since been abandoned, with Netscape's release of version 6.0. Layers are essentially two-dimensional boxes of content that can be absolutely positioned anywhere on a page. Layers can overlap each other, as well as be made visible or hidden. You can therefore wrap an element in a `<layer>` tag and cause it to appear or disappear using client-side DHTML.

One conflict arises with older Netscape versions in the DOM implementation. Netscape 4.x's DOM specifies the way to access an element with ID `layerID` as follows:

```
document.layers[layerID].visibility = 'show';
```

Listing A.1   Netscape 4.x layer acccess

Note that this is how all elements in the Netscape DOM are accessed, not just layer elements. Conversely, IE 4+ uses the `document.all` method.

```
document.all[layerID].style.visibility = 'visible';
```

Listing A.2   IE's layer access method

Note that, in this case, the way you set the `visibility` style property differs as well.

If you are designing for the W3C-compliant browsers (IE 5+ and Netscape 6.0), you should be using the `document.getElementById` method. This method will work on both browsers.

```
document.getElementById('layerID').style.visibility = 'visible';
```

Listing A.3   Modern browsers

Table A.1 outlines differences that result from the absence of Layers.

Cascading Style Sheets

Cascading Style Sheets (discussed in Chapter 5) were first implemented in Netscape Navigator 4.x and Internet Explorer 4.0, in the form of CSS1. Therefore, if you are writing for earlier-version browsers, you cannot and should not include references to CSS. In general, when we have used CSS in this text, we are referring to a combination of both the CSS1 and CSS2 standards, as defined here.

WHAT IS CSS1?

CSS1 is the first version of CSS, a W3C recommendation published in December 1996. This specification is specifically for customizing content in an organized fashion throughout a document. It is considered a standardized mechanism for allowing developers to attach style attributes such as font and color to a block of HTML.

WHAT IS CSS2?

CSS2 was published as a W3C recommendation in May 1998. It serves as an extension of CSS1; therefore, all parts of CSS2 are backward-compatible with CSS1. It includes specifics such as content positioning, internationalization, and table layout, as well as media-enhanced stylesheets, allowing customization of stylesheets to media-specific devices (such as handheld devices, streaming audio, and streaming video).

KEY RELEASE POINTS

Both IE 5.5 and Netscape 6.0 support CSS1, as well as a significant amount of CSS2. Earlier versions of Netscape and IE supported CSS1, but not without problems. Both IE 4.0 and Netscape 4.x in particular had a lot of bugs (discussed next). IE 4.0 was released later than Netscape 4 (see Figure A.1), so Microsoft benefited from a more developed W3C standard. Some of the more well-known bugs include the following:

* A web page loses its JavaScript or CSS variable information when the browser window is resized or a resize event occurs (Netscape 4.x).
* Disabling JavaScript disables CSS as well (Netscape 4.x).
* Putting an href in front of a stylesheet reference causes the stylesheet to load incorrectly. (Netscape 4.x).
* Style inheritance breaks down upon entering a table element (IE 4.0).
* Style.display property is not supported (IE 4.0).

For a more comprehensive list of CSS bugs, please consult the Code-Notes website at ⊶➙UI090001.

CSS and the DOM

Accessing CSS from the DOM also presents some minor difficulties. Both Netscape 4.x and IE 4.0/5.0 implement a non-W3C implementation for referencing a style's top and left positional properties. The W3C DOM Level 2 specifies that these properties should include a CSS unit suffix (px), as shown in Listing A.4.

```
document.getElementById(objectId).style.left = '50px';
```

Listing A.4   Using style.left *with the DOM*

Both IE 5+ and Netscape 6.0 implement this standard. Therefore, when accessing an element's positional properties, you should parse the string to obtain the actual integer information. See Table A.1 for more details.

Also note that IE's original implementation in 4.0 specified a pixelLeft and pixelTop syntax. This syntax actually still works in IE 5+ and returns a position without requiring the px suffix. However, you should use the `style.top` and `style.left` syntax when accessing an object's positional attributes for cross-browser compatibility.

CSS Validator
The W3C offers a utility to validate your CSS script according to either CSS1 or CSS2 standards. It can be downloaded from the W3C's website at: http://jigsaw.w3.org/css-validator/.

JavaScript

JavaScript is a powerful scripting language for use in web pages. As mentioned in both Chapters 4 ("JavaScript") and 5 ("DHTML and the Document Object Model"), JavaScript has become an almost critical component of most web pages.

KEY RELEASE POINTS

Versions of Navigator Earlier than 2.0 and Versions of IE earlier Than 3.0 Do Not Support JavaScript
JavaScript 1.0 was introduced in Navigator 2.0. IE did not introduce their version, JScript, until IE 3.0. Microsoft's version approximated Navigator's JavaScript in Navigator 2.0, and was therefore roughly a generation behind Netscape (at the time Netscape had already released Navigator 3.0).

Microsoft improved their IE script support with an upgrade to their version 3.0 library, making it compatible with Netscape's 3.0 JavaScript support.

ECMAScript
Both Netscape and IE browsers began supporting a common standard with the release of their respective version 4.0 browsers. Netscape incorporated JavaScript 1.2. Microsoft replied with JScript 3.0 (compatible with JavaScript 1.2). Both browsers supported the standardization to ECMA-262 specifications.

Netscape updated their JavaScript from 1.2 to 1.3 with the release of their 4.7 Navigator. The main features added from JavaScript 1.2 to 1.3 were:

• Internationalization (Unicode support)
• A new Date object specification (this particular object was plat-

form dependent and used platform-specific behavior before the ECMA standardization)

Note that you can specify the version of JavaScript right in your HTML script tag:

```
<script language="JavaScript 1.3">
</script>
```

Listing A.5 Setting JavaScript version

If you specify a version that your browser does not support, the code is ignored. You can specify `language ="JavaScript"` in IE because its interpreter can understand a JavaScript script written for Netscape.

RECENT RELEASES

Both Netscape 6.0 and IE 5.5 provide support for ECMA-262 Revision 3 (the latest version). In Netscape's case, this refers to their JavaScript 1.5. For IE, this is JScript 5.5, which maps cleanly to JavaScript 1.5.

The following major features were introduced with JavaScript 1.5 and JScript 5.5 (and thus only with IE 5.5 and Netscape 6.0):

- Multiple try/catch blocks (see Chapter 4, "JavaScript" topic, "How and Why")
- Runtime errors reported as exceptions that can be caught in a catch block

Therefore, you must be wary of introducing try/catch exception handling. It is supported only by IE 5.5+ and Netscape 6+ browsers.

HTML

KEY RELEASE POINTS

The most recent W3C release of the HTML standard is HTML 4.0. The major differences between this and the prior release of HTML 3.2 are as follows:

- Recognition of both standard and in-line frames.
- Adoption of `object` element, providing a generic tag for working with multimedia.
- Enhancement of table element: columns can be grouped together; header, body, and footer elements are introduced.
- Form enhancements, specifically, tab indexes (allowing users to navigate easily through form fields) and access keys (allowing users to access a specific field in a form with a key press).
- Enhanced event handling (most HTML elements support a wide range of event attributes).
- Enforcement of Document Type Definitions (DTDs).

HTML 4.0 is implemented in IE 4+ and Netscape 6.0.

Compatibility Tables

Table A.1 lists many of the common differences between Netscape, Internet Explorer, and the relevant W3C recommendation.

Netscape 4.x	IE 4/5	W3C Recommendation
document.layers[]	document.all	document.getElementById
element.visibility	*element*.style.visibility	*element*.style.visibility
element.left	*element*.style.pixelLeft	parseInt(*element*.style.left)
element.top	*element*.style.pixelTop	parseInt(*element*.style.top)
LAYER	—	DIV
ILAYER	—	IFRAME

Table A.1   Netscape IE W3C differences

Table A.2 lists levels of support for different versions of Internet Explorer and Netscape.

	DHTML Support	ECMA Script	CSS	DOM Syntax	Technologies Introduced	HTML
IE 6.0 (beta)	DOM Level 1	1.5	CSS2 (partial) CSS1	document. getElementById document.all	SmartTags .NET Integration Enhanced element support	HTML 4.0

	DHTML Support	ECMA Script	CSS	DOM Syntax	Technologies Introduced	HTML
IE 5.5	DOM Level 1 (partial)	1.5	CSS1	document. getElementById document.all	DHTML Element behaviors Enhanced CSS1 support Print-preview	HTML 4.0
IE 5.0	DOM Level 1 (partial)	1.3	CSS1	document. getElementById document.all	Enhanced CSS support W3C DOM support DHTML behaviors	HTML 4.0
IE 4.0	Non-W3C-compliant	1.2	CSS1 (partial)	document.all	DHTML Channels Active desktop	HTML 4.0
IE 3.0	—	1.0 / 1.1	CSS1 (partial)	—	Stylesheets JScript ActiveX Enhanced video/audio multimedia	HTML 3.2
IE 2.0	—	—	—	—	Frames (v. 2.1) SSL HTTP cookies OLE	HTML 2.0/3.0
Netscape 6.0	DOM Level 1	1.5	CSS2 (partial) CSS1	document. getElementById	Excellent standards support Enhanced interface	HTML 4.0
Netscape 4.x	Non-W3C-compliant	1.2 / 1.3	CSS1	document.layers	DHTML Layers Enhanced event model	HTML 3.2
Netscape 3.0	—	1.1	—	—	Image rollovers (via scripting) Enhanced table support	HTML 3.2
Netscape 2.0		1.0	—	—	JavaScript SSL Frames	IITML 2.0/3.0

Table A.2   Browser compatibility

Table A.3 illustrates some of the differences in IE's event model, compared to the W3C standard used by Netscape 6.0.

Property Description	W3C Implementation	IE (window.event)
Determine the node the target event originated from		srcElement
Determine the node the handler is assigned to Cancel the current event	currentTarget stopPropagation()	No implementation. (use the *this* keyword to determine the current node) cancelBubble (boolean set true)

Table A.3   Cross-platform event support

Timeline

Figure A.1 shows a brief timeline of the various browser releases. This timeline can be a useful tool in determining which generation of browsers supports which level of standard.

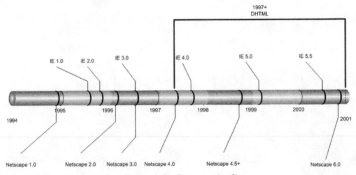

Figure A.1   Browser timeline

Index